KT-499-290

CONTENTS

Introduction (v)

Question and Answer bank	Questions	Answers
Chapter Tasks		
1 Managing the granting of credit	3	61
2 Granting credit to customers	8	63
3 Legislation and credit control	27	71
4 Methods of credit control	36	75
5 Managing the supply of credit	44	79
AAT AQ2013 Sample Assessment	89	115
BPP Practice Assessment 1	131	161
BPP Practice Assessment 2	173	201

A NOTE ABOUT COPYRIGHT

Dear Customer

What does the little © mean and why does it matter?

Your market-leading BPP books, course materials and e-learning materials do not write and update themselves. People write them: on their own behalf or as employees of an organisation that invests in this activity. Copyright law protects their livelihoods. It does so by creating rights over the use of the content.

Breach of copyright is a form of theft – as well being a criminal offence in some jurisdictions, it is potentially a serious breach of professional ethics.

With current technology, things might seem a bit hazy but, basically, without the express permission of BPP Learning Media:

- Photocopying our materials is a breach of copyright

- Scanning, ripcasting or conversion of our digital materials into different file formats, uploading them to facebook or emailing them to your friends is a breach of copyright

You can, of course, sell your books, in the form in which you have bought them – once you have finished with them. (Is this fair to your fellow students? We update for a reason.) Please note the e-products are sold on a single user licence basis: we do not supply 'unlock' codes to people who have bought them secondhand.

And what about outside the UK? BPP Learning Media strives to make our materials available at prices students can afford by local printing arrangements, pricing policies and partnerships which are clearly listed on our website. A tiny minority ignore this and indulge in criminal activity by illegally photocopying our material or supporting organisations that do. If they act illegally and unethically in one area, can you really trust them?

This book is to be re

AAT

Qualifications and Credit Framework (QCF)

AQ2013
LEVEL 4 DIPLOMA IN ACCOUNTING

(QCF)

QUESTION BANK

College of North West London
Wembley Park Learning Resources Centre
Crescent House
130-140 Wembley Park Drive HA9 8HP

Credit Control

2013 Edition

627040

627040   658,88 : Accounting; RDP

First edition June 2013
ISBN 9781 4727 0355 2

British Library Cataloguing-in-Publication Data
A catalogue record for this book is available from the British Library

Published by
BPP Learning Media Ltd
BPP House
Aldine Place
London W12 8AA

www.bpp.com/learningmedia

Printed in the United Kingdom by Martins of Berwick
Sea View Works
Spittal
Berwick-Upon-Tweed
TD15 1RS

Your learning materials, published by BPP Learning Media Ltd, are printed on paper obtained from traceable sustainable sources.

All our rights reserved. No part of this publication may be reproduced, stored in a retrieval system or transmitted, in any form or by any means, electronic, mechanical, photocopying, recording or otherwise, without the prior written permission of BPP Learning Media Ltd.

The contents of this book are intended as a guide and not for professional advice. Although every effort has been made to ensure that the contents of this book are correct at the time of going to press, BPP Learning Media makes no warranty that the information in this book is accurate or complete and accepts no liability for any loss or damaged suffered by any person acting or refraining from acting as a result of the material in this book.

We are grateful to the AAT for permission to reproduce the AAT sample assessment(s). The answers to the AAT sample assessment(s) have been published by the AAT. All other answers have been prepared by BPP Learning Media Ltd.

©
BPP Learning Media Ltd
2013

INTRODUCTION

This is BPP Learning Media's AAT Question Bank for Credit Control. It is part of a suite of ground-breaking resources produced by BPP Learning Media for the AAT's assessments under the Qualification and Credit Framework.

The Credit Control assessment will be **computer assessed**. As well as being available in the traditional paper format, this **Question Bank is available in an online environment** containing tasks similar to those you will encounter in the AAT's testing environment. BPP Learning Media believe that the best way to practise for an online assessment is in an online environment. However, if you are unable to practise in the online environment you will find that the tasks in the paper Question Bank have been written in a style that is as close as possible to the style that you will be presented with in your online assessment.

This Question Bank has been written in conjunction with the BPP Text, and has been carefully designed to enable students to practise all of the learning outcomes and assessment criteria for the units that make up Credit Control. It is fully up to date as at June 2013 and reflects both the AAT's unit guide and the sample assessment(s) provided by the AAT.

This Question Bank contains these key features:

- tasks corresponding to each chapter of the Text. Some tasks are designed for learning purposes, others are of assessment standard

- the AAT's sample assessment(s) and answers for Credit Control and further BPP practice assessments

The emphasis in all tasks and assessments is on the practical application of the skills acquired.

VAT

You may find tasks throughout this Question Bank that need you to calculate or be aware of a rate of VAT. This is stated at 20% in these examples and questions.

Approaching the assessment

When you sit the assessment it is very important that you follow the on screen instructions. This means you need to carefully read the instructions, both on the introduction screens and during specific tasks.

When you access the assessment you should be presented with an introductory screen with information similar to that shown below (taken from the introductory screen from the AAT's Sample Assessment for Credit Control).

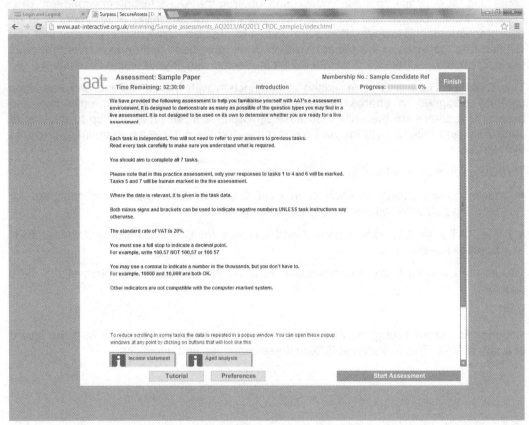

The actual instructions will vary depending on the subject you are studying for. It is very important you read the instructions on the introductory screen and apply them in the assessment. You don't want to lose marks when you know the correct answer just because you have not entered it in the right format.

In general, the rules set out in the AAT Sample Assessments for the subject you are studying for will apply in the real assessment, but you should again read the information on this screen in the real assessment carefully just to make sure. This screen may also confirm the VAT rate used if applicable.

A full stop is needed to indicate a decimal point. We would recommend using minus signs to indicate negative numbers and leaving out the comma signs to indicate thousands, as this results in a lower number of key strokes and less margin for error when working under time pressure. Having said that, you can use whatever is easiest for you as long as you operate within the rules set out for your particular assessment.

You have to show competence in all sections of assessments and you should therefore complete all of the tasks. Don't leave questions unanswered.

In some assessments written or complex tasks may be human marked. In this case you are given a blank space or table to enter your answer into. You should be told in the assessments which tasks these are (note: there may be none if all answers are marked by the computer).

If these involve calculations, it is a good idea to decide in advance how you are going to lay out your answers to such tasks by practising answering them on a word document, and certainly you should try all such tasks in this question bank and in the AAT's environment using the sample/practice assessments.

When asked to fill in tables, or gaps, never leave any blank even if you are unsure of the answer. Fill in your best estimate.

Note that for some assessments where there is a lot of scenario information or tables of data provided (eg tax tables), you may need to access these via 'pop-ups'. Instructions will be provided on how you can bring up the necessary data during the assessment.

Finally, take note of any task specific instructions once you are in the assessment. For example you may be asked to enter a date in a certain format or to enter a number to a certain number of decimal places.

Remember you can practise the BPP questions in this question bank in an online environment on our dedicated AAT Online page. On the same page is a link to the current AAT Sample Assessments as well.

If you have any comments about this book, please e-mail ianblackmore@bpp.com or write to Ian Blackmore, AAT Product Manager, BPP Learning Media Ltd, BPP House, Aldine Place, London W12 8AA.

Question bank

Chapter 1 Managing the granting of credit

Task 1.1

Which of the following is a cash transaction?

Purchase of non-current assets on an instalment basis ☐

Sale of goods for list price less 2% settlement discount for payment within seven days ☐

Payment of expenses using a company credit card ☐

Sale of non-current assets with terms of 30 days for payment ☐

Task 1.2

There are two main stages of the credit control function – the ordering cycle and the collection cycle.

Consider the following statements:

(i)   A customer receiving an invoice is part of the collection cycle.
(ii) A customer being offered credit is part of the collection cycle.
(iii) A statement sent to a customer is part of the ordering cycle.
(iv) Establishing a customer's credit status is part of the ordering cycle.

The correct statements are:

(i) and (ii) ☐

(ii) and (iv) ☐

(ii) and (iii) ☐

(i) and (iv) ☐

Task 1.3

Which of the following stages in the ordering and collection cycle is least likely to represent a responsibility of the credit control function?

Issuing offer of credit to customer ☐

Issuing invoice to customer ☐

Issuing statement to customer ☐

Issuing payment reminder letter to customer ☐

Task 1.4

The normal credit terms for a business are that payment should be made within 60 days of the invoice date but a settlement discount of 2% is offered for payment within 14 days of the invoice.

How would this be expressed on the sales invoice to the customer?

Net 14/60 days ☐

Gross 60 days net 2% 14 days ☐

Gross 60 days 2% discount for payment within 14 days ☐

Net 60 days 2% discount for payment within 14 days ☐

Task 1.5

Which of the following is not a main role of the credit control department:

The initial decision whether to grant credit ☐

Ongoing checks on credit limits ☐

The pursuit of payment ☐

The despatch of goods ☐

Task 1.6

Which of the following is NOT an external source of information for assessing a customer's credit status?

The Internet ☐

Customer visit ☐

Companies House (for filed financial statements) ☐

Bank reference ☐

Task 1.7

Which of the following would not be classified as a liquid asset?

Receivables ☐

Bank deposit accounts ☐

Non-current assets ☐

Inventory ☐

Task 1.8

What are the two main stages in the credit control function?

Despatch cycle and collection cycle ☐

Ordering cycle and payment cycle ☐

Despatch cycle and payment cycle ☐

Ordering cycle and collection cycle ☐

Task 1.9

Which of the following describes the liquidity of a business?

The ability to make a profit ☐

The ability to pay amounts when they are due ☐

The ability to raise loan finance ☐

The ability to pay a dividend when due ☐

Task 1.10

Which of the following sources of information would be useful in assessing the credit status of a potential new credit customer?

(i)   Bank reference
(ii)   Aged receivables' listing
(iii)   Sales representatives knowledge
(iv)   Credit agency reference
(v)   Trade reference
(vi)   Analysis of recent financial statements

(i), (iv), (v) and (vi) ☐

(ii), (iv), (v) and (vi) ☐

(i), (iii), (iv) and (v) ☐

(ii), (iii), (v) and (vi) ☐

Task 1.11

Which of the following is a credit transaction?

Purchase of goods by cheque ☐

Purchase of a non-current asset in three equal instalments ☐

Sale of goods by credit card ☐

Delivery of goods to customer for cash ☐

Task 1.12

Which of the following is correct?

Despatch of goods is part of the collection cycle. ☐

The customer being offered credit is part of the collection cycle. ☐

Establishing customer credit status is part of the ordering cycle. ☐

A statement sent to a customer is part of the ordering cycle. ☐

Task 1.13

An organisation has credit terms of 30 days but some customers are offered a 2% discount for payment within ten days.

How would these credit terms be disclosed on the customer's invoice?

Gross 30 days Net 20 days 2% ☐

Gross 30 days 2% discount for 10 days ☐

Net 30 days 2 % discount for 10 days ☐

Net 30 days 2% discount for 20 days ☐

Task 1.14

Which of the following sources of information would be useful in determining whether to increase the credit period offered to an existing credit customer?

(i)   Bank reference

(ii)   Aged receivables' listing

(iii) Sales representative's knowledge

(iv) Credit agency reference

(v)   Trade reference

(vi) Analysis of recent financial statements

(ii), (iii), (iv) and (vi) ☐

(i), (ii), (v) and (vi) ☐

(ii), (iii), (v) and (vi) ☐

(i), (iii), (iv) and (v) ☐

Chapter 2 Granting credit to customers

Task 2.1

Which of the following would NOT be a normal method of establishing the creditworthiness of potential new customers?

Aged receivables' analysis ☐

Bank reference ☐

Credit reference agency ☐

Supplier reference ☐

Task 2.2

Which of the following are external sources of information about a company requesting credit from your business?

Supplier reference, credit reference agency, aged receivables' analysis ☐

Bank reference, aged receivables' analysis, Companies House ☐

Supplier reference, personal visit, bank reference ☐

Bank reference, Companies House, credit reference agency ☐

Task 2.3

Which of the following are valid reasons for deciding not to grant credit to a new customer?

(i)   Adverse press reports about the customer
(ii) A non-committal bank reference
(iii) Lack of financial statements due to being a recently started company

(i) and (ii) ☐

(i) and (iii) ☐

(ii) and (iii) ☐

All of the above ☐

Task 2.4

A business has a gross profit of £125,000 and an operating profit (profit from operations) of £60,000. The annual revenue was £500,000 and the total net assets of the business were £600,000.

Calculate the following ratios:

Gross profit margin	
Operating profit margin	
Return on capital employed	
Net asset turnover	

Task 2.5

Given below is an extract from the statement of financial position of a business:

	£'000	£'000
Non-current assets		1,200
Current assets:		
Inventory	80	
Trade receivables	120	
Cash	10	
	210	
Current liabilities:		
Trade payables	100	
Tax	8	
	108	
Net current assets		102
		1,302
Long-term loans		(500)
		802

The summarised statement of profit or loss for the year is:

	£'000
Sales revenue	750
Cost of sales	(500)
Gross profit	250
Operating expenses	(180)
Finance costs (interest paid)	(40)
Profit before tax	30
Tax	(8)
Profit for the year	22

Calculate the following accounting ratios:

Current ratio	
Quick ratio	
Inventory holding period	
Accounts receivable collection period	
Accounts payable payment period	
Return on capital employed	
Gearing ratio	
Interest cover	

··

Task 2.6

You are the credit controller for a business which has received a request for £20,000 of credit from a potential new customer, Faverly Ltd. Faverly Ltd has provided you with its latest set of financial statements which are summarised as follows:

BPP
LEARNING MEDIA

Statement of profit or loss for the year ended 30 June

	20X8	20X7
	£'000	£'000
Sales revenue	2,400	2,250
Cost of sales	(1,870)	(1,770)
Gross profit	530	480
Operating expenses	(230)	(210)
Operating profit	300	270
Finance costs (interest payable)	(70)	(48)
Profit before tax	230	222
Taxation	(57)	(55)
Profit after tax	173	167

Statements of financial position as at 30 June

	20X8	20X7
	£'000	£'000
ASSETS		
Non-current assets	3,200	2,867
Current assets		
Inventory	264	216
Trade receivables	336	360
	600	576
Total assets	3,800	3,443
EQUITY AND LIABILITIES		
Equity		
Share capital	1,500	1,500
Retained earnings	1,196	1,083
Total equity	2,696	2,583
Current liabilities		
Trade payables	384	380
Bank overdraft	720	480
Total liabilities	1,104	860
Total equity and liabilities	3,800	3,443

You have also received a bank reference from Faverly Ltd's bank which reads "should prove good for your figures".

Finally, you have received the following trade references:

We have received a request for credit from Faverly Ltd who have quoted yourselves as a referee. We would be grateful if you could answer the following questions and return in the stamped addressed envelope enclosed.

How long has the customer been trading with you?	Three years six months
Your credit terms with customer per month	£10,000
Period of credit granted	30 days
Payment record	Prompt/occasionally late/slow
Have you ever suspended credit to the customer?	Yes/No
If yes – when and for how long?	20X6 for six months
Any other relevant information	

We have received a request for credit from Faverly Ltd who have quoted yourselves as a referee. We would be grateful if you could answer the following questions and return in the stamped addressed envelope enclosed.

How long has the customer been trading with you?	Five years three months
Your credit terms with customer per month	£10,000
Period of credit granted	30 days
Payment record	Prompt/occasionally late/slow
Have you ever suspended credit to the customer?	Yes/No
Any other relevant information	

BPP
LEARNING MEDIA

You are required to carry out an assessment of the information provided for Faverly Ltd and to record your results and recommendation as to whether credit of £20,000 should be extended to Faverly Ltd in a memo to the finance director of your business.

Task 2.7

You are the credit controller for a business and you have received a request from Fisher Ltd for credit of £15,000 from your company on a 30-day basis. Two trade references have been provided but no bank reference. You have also received the last set of published financial statements which include the previous year's comparative figures.

The trade references appeared satisfactory although one is from Froggett & Sons and it has been noted that the managing director of Fisher Ltd is Mr N Froggett. Analysis of the financial statements has indicated a decrease in profitability during the last year, a high level of gearing and fairly low liquidity ratios.

Draft a letter to the finance director of Fisher Ltd on the basis that credit is to be currently refused but may be extended once the most recent financial statements have been examined.

Task 2.8

Which of the following would be possible reasons for the refusal of credit to a new customer?

(i)   A non-committal or poor bank reference
(ii)   Not having traded with the customer before
(iii)   Concerns about the validity of any trade references submitted
(iv)   Adverse press comment about the potential customer
(v)   Customer is in a different line of business to most customers

(ii), (iii) and (iv) ☐

(i), (ii) and (v) ☐

(i), (iii) and (iv) ☐

(ii), (iv) and (v) ☐

Task 2.9

The following statements relate to EBITDA, a figure which is sometimes used in financial analysis calculations:

(i) EBITDA stands for Earnings before Interest, Tax, Dividends and Amortisation.

(ii) EBITDA removes some of the subjectivity from the profit figure that arises as a result of management and accounting policies.

Which of the following is the correct description of the accuracy of these statements?

Statement (i)	Statement (ii)	✓
True	False	
True	True	
False	False	
False	True	

Task 2.10

You are employed as an assistant accountant in Fastover Ltd. Your company's financial controller wants you to assess the creditworthiness of Whittle Ltd. Whittle Ltd has placed a large order with your company and any problems paying would have an impact on your company's cash flow.

You have a copy of Fastover Ltd's credit control procedures manual which sets guidelines on when credit should be granted. Extracts are set out below.

Extract from procedures manual

Extending credit to new customers

The supply of goods/services on credit necessarily involves risk. To minimise that risk the following steps should be taken before extending credit to a new customer.

1. Two references from independent referees should be obtained. Any problems raised by the references should be followed-up and further references should be taken, if appropriate.

2. The latest set of financial statements of a company should be obtained and ratio analysis undertaken. Any problems raised by the analysis should be followed-up.

3. Assuming points 1 and 2 are satisfactory, a credit limit should be set by the Credit Control Manager. This should initially be a very conservative limit which is closely monitored. The limit may be reviewed after six months.

You have also received the following references from two of Whittle Ltd's suppliers and extracts from Whittle Ltd's financial statements over the last two years.

FASTOVER LTD

11 Beal Street

Wallington

WL1 9PO

Tel: 0331 8676767

5 January 20X8

PRIVATE AND CONFIDENTIAL

Credit Manager

Greatlygrow Ltd

Long Street

Wallington

WL7 9ZW

Dear Sir or Madam

We have recently received a request from a customer of ours, Whittle Ltd, giving yourselves as a reference. We would be grateful if you would answer the following questions and return them in the enclosed stamped addressed envelope.

1.   For how long has Whittle Ltd been trading with you?

One year

2.   Did you take up references for Whittle Ltd when you began trading with them?

Two references

3.   How long a credit period do you normally extend to Whittle Ltd?

Six weeks

4.   Does Whittle Ltd make payments in accordance with credit terms?

Yes

5.   Have you ever suspended credit being extended to Whittle Ltd?

No

If YES please give date and period of suspension.

6.   Please supply any information which you consider relevant.

Thank you for your help.

Yours faithfully

Brian Herbert

Brian Herbert – Credit Control Manager

BPP
LEARNING MEDIA

FASTOVER LTD

11 Beal Street

Wallington

WL1 9PO

Tel: 0331 8676767

5 January 20X8

PRIVATE AND CONFIDENTIAL

Credit Manager

Weston Ltd

Weston Court

Wallington, WL5 8PP

Dear Sir or Madam

We have recently received a request from a customer of ours, Whittle Ltd, giving yourselves as a reference. We would be grateful if you would answer the following questions and return them in the enclosed stamped addressed envelope.

1. For how long has Whittle Ltd been trading with you?

Five years

2. Did you take up references for Whittle Ltd when you began trading with them?

Two references

3. How long a credit period do you normally extend to Whittle Ltd?

Two months

4. Does Whittle Ltd make payments in accordance with credit terms?

Usually

5. Have you ever suspended credit being extended to Whittle Ltd?

Yes

If YES please give date and period of suspension.

Once, two years ago for six months

6. Please supply any information which you consider relevant.

Thank you for your help.

Yours faithfully

Brian Herbert

Brian Herbert – Credit Control Manager

Extracts from the financial statements of Whittle Ltd

Statements of financial position

	This year £	Last year £
ASSETS		
Non-current assets		
Intangible assets	200	180
Tangible non-current assets	790	670
Investments	900	600
	1,890	1,450
Current assets		
Inventories	200	170
Trade receivables	800	750
Cash	90	105
	1,090	1,025
Total assets	2,980	2,475
EQUITY AND LIABILITIES		
Equity		
Called-up share capital	1,000	1,000
Retained earnings	510	117
Total equity	1,510	1,117
Non-current liabilities		
Borrowings	500	400
Current liabilities		
Trade payables	900	890
Other	70	68
	970	958
Total liabilities	1,470	1,358
Total equity and liabilities	2,980	2,475

Statement of profit or loss extract

Profit after interest and taxation	500	190

Using the information given and bearing in mind the guidelines in the quality control procedures manual, recommend in a memo to the financial controller whether Whittle Ltd should have credit terms extended to it.

Your ratio analysis should include the following ratios:

- Current ratio
- Quick ratio (or acid test ratio)
- Gearing ratio

Task 2.11

You work as an accounting technician for Sleepy Ltd. You have recently received a request for credit facilities from the finance director of Dreams Ltd. The company has supplied its statement of profit or loss for the year ended 30 June 20X8. In addition, in accordance with the credit policy of Sleepy Ltd, trade references have been obtained from two of Dreams Ltd's suppliers, Carpets Ltd and Wardrobes Ltd. The request for credit, statement of profit or loss and references are as follows.

DREAMS LTD
17 High Street
Newport
South Wales

Mr S Wilks
Financial Controller

Sleepy Ltd
Tregarn Trading Estate
Cardiff
CF1 3EW   21 December 20X8

Dear Mr Wilks

We are a long-established company and trade as a retailer of furniture. We are keen to do business with your company. In order to facilitate this we would be grateful if you could confirm that you will be able to provide us with £20,000 of credit on 60 days terms.

I enclose a copy of our latest audited statement of profit or loss. You may also wish to contact two of our existing suppliers for trade references. I would suggest the following two:

Carpets Ltd
Monnow Way

Bristol
BS7 6TY
Wardrobes Ltd
Pansy Park
Liverpool
L4 1HQ

I look forward to hearing from you shortly.

Yours sincerely

D Jones

David Jones – Finance director

CARPETS LTD

MONNOW WAY

BRISTOL

BS7 6TY

Pat King

Accounting Technician

Sleepy Ltd

Tregarn Trading Estate

Cardiff

CF1 3EW   28 December 20X8

Dear Sir/Madam

In response to your request for credit information on Dreams Ltd our response is as follows:

- We have traded with the company for four years.

- We allow the company £10,000 of credit on 30-day terms.

- We find that on average the company takes 60 days to settle their account with us.

- We are not aware of any other information which you should consider.

Yours faithfully

A Evans

Anne Evans – Credit Controller

WARDROBES LTD

Pansy Park

Liverpool

L4 1HQ

Pat King
Accounting Technician
Sleepy Ltd
Tregarn Trading Estate
Cardiff
CF1 3EW

28 December 20X8

Dear Sir/Madam

In response to your request for credit information on Dreams Ltd our response is as follows:

- We have traded with the company for three months.
- We allow the company £2,500 of credit on 30 days terms.
- The company settles its account with us in accordance with our credit terms.
- We are not aware of any other information which you should consider.

Yours faithfully

J Corkhill

J Corkhill – Credit Controller

Dreams Ltd

Statement of profit or loss for the year ended 30 June

	20X8	20X7
	£'000	£'000
Sales revenue	1,800	1,750
Cost of sales	(1,250)	(1,190)
Gross profit	550	560
Net operating expenses	(500)	(550)
Operating profit	50	10
Finance costs	(30)	(20)
Profit/(loss) before taxation	20	(10)
Taxation	–	3
Profit/(loss) for the year after taxation	20	(7)

BPP LEARNING MEDIA

(a) **Prepare a memo setting out any concerns you have in connection with the request. You should include an analysis of the statement of profit or loss of Dreams Ltd and refer to the trade references.**

(b) **Draft a letter to Mr D Jones at Dreams Ltd in reply to the original request for credit facilities.**

Task 2.12

If the accounts receivable collection period is greater than the accounts payable payment period this will mean which of the following for a business?

The business is making a profit.

The business is making a loss.

Cash is going out of the business more quickly than it is coming in.

Cash is coming into the business more quickly than it is going out.

Task 2.13

Consider each of the following statements:

(i)   The granting of credit can result in lost interest to a business
(ii)   The granting of credit can increase sales
(iii)   The granting of credit can decrease irrecoverable debts

Which of the statements are correct?

(i) and (ii) only

(i) and (iii) only

(ii) and (iii) only

All three

Task 2.14

What question would not normally be asked when requesting a trade reference from a supplier of a potential new credit customer?

Have you ever suspended credit to this customer?

How long have you been trading with this customer?

Do you think this customer has a good reputation?

What level of credit do you allow this customer?

Task 2.15

A company has a gross profit of £298,000 and an operating profit of £149,000. Share capital is £400,000, reserves total £380,000 and there is a long-term loan of £150,000.

What is the return on capital employed?

28.1% ☐

19.1% ☐

32.0% ☐

16.0% ☐

Task 2.16

Which of the following is a disadvantage of management accounts compared to financial accounts as a means of assessing a prospective credit customer?

They are more up-to-date. ☐

They show the information that management feels important. ☐

They are not in a set format therefore can be tailored to the organisation. ☐

They are not audited. ☐

Task 2.17

The use of EBITDA rather than profit before interest when calculating ratios for an organisation has the following advantage.

The calculation is simpler. ☐

The figure is a closer approximation to profit. ☐

The figure gives an idea of the gearing of the organisation. ☐

The figure gives a closer approximation to cash flow. ☐

Task 2.18

Which of the following would not be included in a letter of refusal of credit to a potential new credit customer?

Offer of cash trading ☐

Offer of future reassessment of creditworthiness ☐

Details of supplier references ☐

Concerns about financial statements ☐

Chapter 3 Legislation and credit control

Task 3.1

What are the three fundamental elements of a contract?

Consideration, offer, acceptance ☐

Intention to create legal relations, consideration, agreement ☐

Invitation to treat, offer, acceptance ☐

Offer, acceptance, intention to create legal relations ☐

Task 3.2

Ashley goes into a shop and picks up a newspaper and goes to the cash till to pay for it.

What element of the contract is this?

Invitation to treat ☐

Consideration ☐

Offer ☐

Acceptance ☐

Task 3.3

In contract law an offer can be brought to an end in a variety of different ways.

Which of the following are ways in which an offer can be brought to an end?

(i)   Revocation of the offer
(ii) Legal action
(iii) A counter-offer
(iv) Lapse of set period of time
(v)   Silence

(i), (iii) and (iv) ☐

(ii), (iii) and (v) ☐

(i), (iii) and (v) ☐

(i), (iv) and (v) ☐

Task 3.4

A term in a contract is fundamental to the contract and if it is broken then the party breaking the term will be in breach of contract and can be sued for damages and the injured party can terminate the contract if they wish.

What is the name given to this type of term?

Express term ☐

Implied term ☐

Warranty ☐

Condition ☐

Task 3.5

There are a variety of possible remedies for a breach of contract.

Which of these remedies is most appropriate for a seller of goods where the buyer has not paid?

Monetary damages ☐

Action for the price ☐

Specific performance ☐

Injunction ☐

Task 3.6

An action is to be brought to court against a receivable for non-payment of an amount of £7,500.

Which court should the action be brought in?

Small Claims Court ☐

High Court ☐

Employment Tribunal ☐

County Court ☐

BPP
LEARNING MEDIA

Task 3.7

A business is owed £20,000 from a receivable and the court has ordered a warrant of execution.

What is a warrant of execution?

The business will be paid the amount owing directly by the receivable's employer as a certain amount is deducted from their weekly/monthly pay. ☐

The business will be paid directly by a third party. ☐

A court bailiff seizes and sells the receivable's goods on behalf of the business. ☐

The receivable makes regular, agreed payments into court to pay off the debt. ☐

Task 3.8

What is a statutory demand?

A method of payment similar to a standing order ☐

A demand for payment from an outstanding receivable of £750 or more ☐

A demand from the tax authorities for payment ☐

A demand for payment of interest on outstanding amounts for a receivable ☐

Task 3.9

If a customer is declared bankrupt what is the order in which their assets are used to make payments due?

Secured creditors, unsecured creditors, bankruptcy costs, preferential creditors ☐

Preferential creditors, secured creditors, bankruptcy costs, unsecured creditors ☐

Preferential creditors, secured creditors, unsecured creditors, bankruptcy costs ☐

Secured creditors, bankruptcy costs, preferential creditors, unsecured creditors ☐

Task 3.10

In a liquidation, a company is dissolved and the assets are realised with debts being paid out of the proceeds and any excess being returned to the shareholders.

In this process by what term are the trade payables of the liquidated business known as?

Secured creditors with floating charge ☐

Preferential creditors ☐

Unsecured creditors ☐

Secured creditors with fixed charge ☐

Task 3.11

A company is insolvent when it cannot pay its debts as they fall due.

Which of the following is not a route for a payable to recover the amounts due?

Administration ☐

Bankruptcy ☐

Receivership ☐

Liquidation ☐

Task 3.12

Under the Data Protection Act what is meant by a data subject?

A person who holds personal information ☐

A company whose data is held ☐

A person who processes personal information ☐

An individual whose data is held ☐

Task 3.13

Under the Sale of Goods Act goods are expected to be "fit for purpose".

What is meant by "fit for purpose"?

They are fully functioning. ☐

They are of satisfactory quality. ☐

They are what they are described to be. ☐

They do what they are expected to do. ☐

Task 3.14

What is the correct formula for calculating interest under the Late Payment of Commercial Debts Act?

Net Debt × (base rate + 8%) / 365 ☐

Net Debt × (base rate + 8%) × (No. of days overdue / 365) ☐

Gross Debt × (base rate + 8%) / 365 ☐

Gross Debt × (base rate + 8%) × (No. of days overdue / 365) ☐

Task 3.15

There are three tracks for recovering debts in the County Court. Which of the following is not a track?

Multi-track ☐

Fast track ☐

Slow track ☐

Small claims track ☐

Task 3.16

Which of the following statements is correct?

(i) The parties to a social or domestic arrangement are presumed to have intended the arrangement to be legally enforceable.

(ii) The parties to a commercial transaction are presumed **not** to have intended the arrangement to be legally enforceable.

(i) only ☐

(ii) only ☐

Both (i) and (ii) ☐

Neither (i) nor (ii) ☐

Task 3.17

Which of the following statements is correct?

Consideration:

(i) Must be of adequate and sufficient value

(ii) Must come from the promisee

(i) only ☐

(ii) only ☐

Both (i) and (ii) ☐

Neither (i) or (ii) ☐

BPP
LEARNING MEDIA

Task 3.18

Which of the following is an offer?

An advertisement in the newsagent's window ☐

An invitation to tender ☐

An auction bid ☐

An exhibition of goods for sale ☐

Task 3.19

Which of the following are essential requirements of a contract?

(i)   Offer and acceptance
(ii) Consideration
(iii) Written contractual terms
(iv) Intention to create legal relations

(i), (ii), (iii) and (iv) ☐

(i), (ii) and (iii) ☐

(i), (ii) and (iv) ☐

(i), (iii) and (iv) ☐

Task 3.20

Which one of the following types of term is stated in a contract and is binding on both parties?

Express terms ☐

Implied terms ☐

Allowed terms ☐

Intended terms ☐

Task 3.21

Under the Data Protection Act how many principles of good practice are there?

5 ☐

8 ☐

10 ☐

12 ☐

Task 3.22

Alexander wrote to Brian and offered to sell him his set of antique cigarette cards for £300. Brian wrote back that he accepted the offer and would pay for them in two instalments of £150.

Is there a contract?

Yes. There is offer, acceptance and consideration. The contract is valid. ☐

No. Alexander's letter was not an offer but an invitation to treat. ☐

No. Until Alexander receives Brian's letter, the acceptance is not valid. ☐

No. Brian's letter has varied the terms and so is a counter-offer, rejecting Alexander's original offer. ☐

Task 3.23

Consider the following statements:

(i) The parties to a social or domestic agreement are presumed to have intended the agreement to be legally enforceable.

(ii) The parties to a commercial agreement are presumed to have intended the arrangement to be legally enforceable.

Which statements are true?

(i) only ☐

(ii) only ☐

Both (i) and (ii) ☐

Neither statement ☐

Task 3.24

Which of the following best describes consideration?

The promise of an exchange of value ☐

The payment of cash ☐

The intention for the parties to be legally bound ☐

The creation of a fair contract ☐

Chapter 4 Methods of credit control

Task 4.1

A business has normal credit terms of payment within 60 days of the invoice date. It is considering offering a settlement discount of 1% for payment within ten days of the invoice date.

What is the approximate annual cost of this discount?

1% ☐

0.74% ☐

7.4% ☐

73.7% ☐

Task 4.2

Widmerpool Ltd makes sales to certain customers of £100,000 with an average collection period of two months. Kenneth, its managing director, is considering whether to introduce a discount of 3% on sales to these customers in return for immediate cash settlement. Widmerpool normally requires a 15% return on its investments.

What is the cost of the discount and would it be worth introducing?

Cost	Introduce or not?	
18.8%	Yes	☐
3.8%	Yes	☐
18.8%	No	☐
3.8%	No	☐

Task 4.3

Brickwood grants credit terms of 60 days net to its major customers, but offers an early settlement discount of 2.5% for payment within seven days.

What is the cost of the discount?

17.7% ☐

17.2% ☐

15.6% ☐

2.5% ☐

Task 4.4

Herbage Ltd is proposing to increase the credit period it gives to customers from one calendar month to two calendar months in order to increase revenue from the present annual figure of £18 million. The price of the product is £10 and it costs £6.40 to make. The increase in the credit period is likely to generate an extra 60,000 unit sales per year. The bank interest cost to the company is 15%.

What is the total financing cost of this policy?

£24,000 ☐

£240,000 ☐

£1,500,000 ☐

£1,600,000 ☐

Task 4.5

Which of the following is not a service provided by a debt factor?

Administration of the receivables ledger ☐

Despatch of goods ☐

Advance of funds ☐

Insurance against irrecoverable debts ☐

Task 4.6

Consider the following statements:

(i)   Invoice discounting is where the book value of the company's receivables are advanced to the company.

(ii) Under an invoice discounting agreement the company collects the debts itself and repays the invoice discounter out of the proceeds.

Which statements are true:

(i) only ☐

(ii) only ☐

(i) and (ii) ☐

Neither statement ☐

Task 4.7

Invoice discounting is a method where

A business offers a discounted price for goods to customers who buy in bulk ☐

A business offers a discounted price for customers who pay invoices early ☐

A business offers a discounted price to customers who buy sub-standard goods ☐

A business lends money to a customer based on a discounted value of the invoices that customer has issued ☐

Task 4.8

The purpose of credit insurance is to allow a business to:

Claim back the legal costs of any court proceedings brought against it by its creditors ☐

Claim back amounts owed to it by customers who have defaulted ☐

Claim back the costs of employing temporary staff to undertake debt collection in the event that the credit controller is on long term sick leave ☐

Continue to meet the interest payments on its loans in the event that it becomes loss-making ☐

Task 4.9

80% of the receivables of a business have been insured for their entire amount and any claim on these receivables would be paid in full.

What type of insurance policy is this?

Annual aggregate excess policy ☐

Partial turnover policy ☐

Specific receivables policy ☐

Whole turnover policy ☐

Task 4.10

Consider the following statements:

(i) A credit collection agency is a commercial organisation providing background information and credit status information about companies and individuals.

(ii) A credit collection agency advances a certain percentage of the carrying amount (book value) of receivables to a business and then takes over the collection of those receivables.

Which of the following correctly describes the accuracy of the statements?

Statement (i)	Statement (ii)	✓
True	True	
True	False	
False	True	
False	False	

Task 4.11

Consider the following statements regarding factoring services:

(i)   With recourse factoring means that the factor bears the risk of irrecoverable debts.

(ii) Factoring is viewed as a normal business operation and will not affect the relationship between the business and its credit customers.

Which of the statements is true?

(i) only ☐

(ii) only ☐

Both statements ☐

Neither statement ☐

Task 4.12

A business currently trades on 30-day credit terms but is considering offering a settlement discount of 1.5% for payment within 14 days of the invoice date.

What is the annual cost of this settlement discount and if the company's bank interest cost is 6% would it be worthwhile to offer the discount?

Cost	Worthwhile?	
3.5%	Yes	☐
3.5%	No	☐
34.7%	Yes	☐
34.7%	No	☐

Task 4.13

How do debt collection agencies normally charge for their services?

A flat fee up front ☐

A monthly flat rate fee ☐

A percentage of amounts collected ☐

A percentage of total receivables ☐

BPP
LEARNING MEDIA

Task 4.14

The provision of finance by a factoring service is a costly but useful service for a business.

Which of the following are likely costs of this provision of finance service?

(i)   Additional interest charged by suppliers on overdue amounts
(ii) Service charge
(iii) Cost of running the receivables ledger
(iv) Additional interest on bank overdraft
(v)   Interest charge on amounts outstanding

(i), (ii) and (v) ☐

(i), (iv) and (v) ☐

(ii), (iii) and (iv) ☐

(ii), (iii) and (v) ☐

Task 4.15

Which of the following is a disadvantage of using the services of a factor?

Cost savings in receivables ledger ☐

Cash advance ☐

Re-instigating receivables ledger ☐

Irrecoverable debt insurance ☐

Task 4.16

Under a whole turnover policy of credit insurance which of the following would be true?

Half of all receivables are covered by the policy. ☐

Irrecoverable debts are insured above an agreed limit. ☐

Specific receivables are insured. ☐

About 80% of receivables are covered for their entire amount. ☐

Task 4.17

A business currently, trades on a basis of one-month credit terms to credit customers. However, the business wishes to increase sales and profits and is considering increasing its credit terms to two months. Currently, the receivables figure of the business is £25,000 and revenue is £300,000. It is anticipated that revenue will increase to £390,000. The business has a net profit percentage of 10% on its sales.

What is the overall profit or loss from this increase in credit terms?

£1,000 profit ☐

£1,000 loss ☐

£4,000 profit ☐

£4,000 loss ☐

Task 4.18

A business currently trades on 60-day credit terms but is considering offering a settlement discount of 3% for payment within 14 days of the invoice date.

What is the annual cost of this settlement discount?

3.0% ☐

80.6% ☐

18.8% ☐

24.5% ☐

Task 4.19

Which of the following are the three main services provided by a factoring service?

(i)   Legal advice

(ii)   Receivables ledger administration

(iii)   Discounting service

(iv) Provision of finance

(v)   Insurance against irrecoverable debts

(i), (iv) and (v)   ☐

(i), (iii) and (iv)   ☐

(ii), (iii) and (v)   ☐

(ii), (iv) and (v)   ☐

Task 4.20

Consider the following statements regarding factoring services:

(i)   If a factor administers the receivables ledger then the factor will be responsible for assessing the credit status of customers.

(ii)   Without recourse factoring means that the business not the factor bears the risk of irrecoverable debts.

Which statements are true?

(i) only   ☐

(ii) only   ☐

Both statements   ☐

Neither statement   ☐

Chapter 5 Managing the supply of credit

Task 5.1

What is a credit customer's credit limit?

The maximum amount the customer can buy on credit each month ☐

The maximum amount of each invoice for goods on credit ☐

The maximum amount the customer can buy on credit each year ☐

The maximum amount allowed to be outstanding at any point in time ☐

Task 5.2

A customer of your business has an outstanding balance on its receivables ledger account of £24,519 at 31 July. This balance is made up as follows:

		£
10 May	Inv 042644	1,473
25 May	Inv 042712	3,265
6 June	Inv 042785	4,273
25 June	Inv 042846	4,175
6 July	Credit note 02764	(400)
10 July	Inv 042913	4,463
16 July	Inv 042962	3,143
25 July	Inv 042987	4,127
		24,519

The customer's name is Knightly Ltd and the company has a credit limit of £30,000.

Complete the aged receivables' analysis given below for this customer as at 31 July.

Total £	Credit limit £	Current, < 30 days £	31 – 60 days £	61 – 90 days £	> 90 days £

BPP LEARNING MEDIA

Task 5.3

Given below is an extract from an aged receivables' analysis for your business at 31 August.

	Total	Credit limit	Current <30 days	31–60 days	61–90 days	> 90 days
	£	£	£	£	£	£
Jeremy Ltd	8,236	10,000	3,757	3,589		890
Lenter Ltd	5,378	8,000	1,873	1,967	1,538	
Friday Partners	400	4,000			400	
Diamond & Co	6,256	5,000	4,227	2,029		

What does the aged receivables' analysis indicate for each of these customers and what action, if any, should be taken?

Task 5.4

You are working in Paddington Ltd's credit control section. The sales manager has asked for your views on the credit status of four organisations to whom Paddington Ltd supplies goods.

Using the extracts from the aged receivables' analysis given below, analyse these four accounts and write a memorandum to the sales manager.

Your memorandum should:

(a) **Provide an opinion of the creditworthiness of the customer and the status of the account**

(b) **Suggest how the account should be managed in the future**

Extract from: Aged receivables' analysis

Customer name and address	Total due	Up to 30 days	Up to 60 days	Up to 90 days	Over 90 days
	£	£	£	£	£
Megacorp plc, Oakham, Rutland	72,540	21,250	12,250	15,500	23,540
Credit limit £85,000.					
Terms of sale: 60 days net.					
Goodfellows Cycles Ltd, Manchester	24,000	19,000			5,000
Credit limit £50,000.					
Terms of sale: 30 days net.					
Hooper-bikes Ltd, Sheffield	26,750	6,250	9,875	5,275	5,350
Credit limit £25,000.					
Terms of sale: 60 days net.					
Dynamo Cycles Ltd Nottingham	2,750	2,750			
Credit limit £7,500.					
Terms of sale: 30 days net.					

....

Task 5.5

Given below is the credit control policy for a business and an extract from its aged receivables' analysis at 30 September.

Credit control policy

1. Invoices must be issued on the same day as goods are despatched.

2. An aged analysis of trade receivables' is to be produced monthly.

3. Credit terms are strictly 30 days from the date of invoice.

4. Statements are despatched on the first working day of each month.

5. A reminder letter must be sent when a debt is 14 days overdue.

6. A telephone call to chase payment must be made when a debt is 21 days overdue.

7. The customer will be placed on the stop list when the amount owing is 30 days overdue and a meeting arranged with the customer to discuss the operation of the account.

8. A letter threatening legal action will be sent when the debt is 45 days overdue.

9. Legal proceedings are to be commenced when a debt is 60 days overdue subject to the agreement of the finance director.

Aged receivables' analysis at 30 September: extract

	Total	Credit limit	Current <30 days	31–60 days	61–90 days	> 90 days
	£	£	£	£	£	£
Carnford Ltd	12,430	15,000				12,430
Luxford Ltd	3,400	4,000	2,500	720		180
KLP Ltd	1,560	2,000		600	960	
Flanders Ltd	18,450	20,000	10,240	6,225	1,985	

For each receivable:

*   **Set out the action to be taken with regard to the customer account**
*   **State how discussion should be conducted if the account is overdue**
*   **Recommend whether any allowances for doubtful debts are required.**

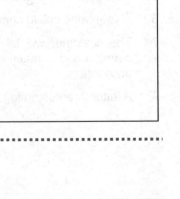

BPP
LEARNING MEDIA

Task 5.6

Draft a first reminder letter to a customer whose debt of £1,350.46 is 14 days overdue.

The customer's name is Harvey Ltd and its account number is 204764.

....

Task 5.7

Draft a letter to a customer whose debt of £976.80 is 30 days overdue and who is to be placed on your business's stop list.

The customer's name is Bart & Sons and its account number is B245.

....

Task 5.8

What is the relevance of the 80/20 rule when dealing with credit control?

Only 80% of receivables' accounts need to considered when analysing the aged receivables listing. ☐

Only the first 80 customers on the aged receivables' listing need to be analysed. ☐

If 20% of the largest customers are analysed this should account for 80% in value. ☐

It is likely that 20% of debts will need to be written-off or an allowance made. ☐

Task 5.9

You are working in the credit control department of Manton Ltd. An extract from the company's aged receivables' analysis at 30 September 20X7, together with information on the transactions that took place during October is shown below.

Prepare an aged receivables' analysis as at 31 October 20X7.

Manton Ltd Aged Receivables' Analysis – 30 September 20X7

Credit terms: 30 days

Customer name and ref	Total amount	Current (< 1 month)	Outstanding 1-2 months	Outstanding 2-3 months	Outstanding >3 months
New Milton	£9,000	£2,000 M89			£7,000 M17
Sway	£1,000	£1,000 M81			
Mudeford	£2,500				£2,500 M24
Barton	£23,000		£13,000 M69	£10,000 M33	
Boscombe	£3,000			£3,000 M38	
TOTAL	**£38,500**	**£3,000**	**£13,000**	**£13,000**	**£9,500**

Transactions during October 20X7:

New Milton	Invoices M17 £7,000 and M89 £2,000 remain unpaid. Invoice M98 £4,000 issued.
Sway	Invoice M81 £1,000 remains unpaid.
Mudeford	Invoice M24 £2,500 paid.
Barton	Paid invoice M33 £10,000. Invoice M69 £13,000 remains unpaid. Invoice M101 £4,000 issued.
Boscombe	Paid invoice M38 £3,000. Invoice M103 £5,000 issued.

BPP LEARNING MEDIA

Task 5.10

Which of the following is the best explanation of materiality in the context of analysing and chasing outstanding debts?

Overdue debts under a certain amount should always be ignored. ☐

Largest debts should be pursued as a first priority with smallest amounts pursued last. ☐

Debts from significant customers should not be chased in such a way as to damage the relationship with the customer. ☐

Outstanding debts that are below a certain limit should be written off without attempts to chase them. ☐

Task 5.11

Frame Ltd's credit controller was sacked recently for failing to implement the company's credit control policies. On analysing the aged receivables you find that Jines Ltd, a customer of Frame Ltd, has not purchased any goods for the last three months and has an amount outstanding of £450 on the receivables ledger.

What action is the most appropriate for you to take in respect of Jines Ltd's debt ?

Telephone Jines Ltd to enquire about the situation in order to determine whether there is any query regarding the amount outstanding and to agree steps for payment ☐

Send Jines Ltd a statement and wait for payment ☐

Suggest that the accounts department writes off Jines Ltd's debt as it is more than 90 days old ☐

Initiate County Court proceedings to recover the debt. ☐

Task 5.12

A customer's outstanding balance at 30 June 20X9 has been analysed as follows:

19/04/X9	Invoice 17563	2,610
23/05/X9	Invoice 17772	1,667
01/06/X9	Credit note 4612	(331)
10/06/X9	Invoice 17890	1,890
21/06/X9	Invoice 17999	1,560
		7,396

The customer has credit terms of 30 days for payment.

What is the total of the amount that is overdue?

£1,667 ☐

£2,610 ☐

£3,119 ☐

£4,277 ☐

BPP
LEARNING MEDIA

Task 5.13

Which of the following is correct?

An irrecoverable debt is one which may or may not be received. ☐

An irrecoverable debt is written off and does not appear in the statement of financial position. ☐

A doubtful debt will likely not be paid. ☐

A doubtful debt is written off and does not appear in the statement of financial position. ☐

Task 5.14

Which of the following would not be part of an organisation's credit control policy?

Setting of credit limits ☐

Inventory ordering ☐

Assessment of credit standing ☐

Collection procedures ☐

Task 5.15

Which of the following information would be required in order to open an account for a new credit customer?

(i)   Credit limit agreed
(ii)   Customer's name and address
(iii) Customer's bank name and address
(iv) Managing Director's name and address
(v)   Payment terms agreed

(i), (ii) and (iv) ☐

(ii), (iii) and (v) ☐

(i), (ii) and (v) ☐

(ii), (iii) and (v) ☐

Task 5.16

A customer has a credit limit of £10,000.

What does this mean?

The customer can spend £10,000 a year on credit.	☐
The customer can spend £10,000 a month on credit.	☐
A single order must not exceed £10,000.	☐
At any point in time the customer's balance must not exceed £10,000.	☐

Task 5.17

Why is it important that a customer's credit limit should not be exceeded?

It is a breach of contract.	☐
It could result in an irrecoverable debt.	☐
Settlement discounts could be cancelled.	☐
Sales may be lost.	☐

Task 5.18

A customer's outstanding balance at 30 June 20X9 has been analysed as follows:

19/04/X9	Invoice 17563	2,610
23/05/X9	Invoice 17772	1,667
01/06/X9	Credit note 4612	(331)
10/06/X9	Invoice 17890	1,890
21/06/X9	Invoice 17999	1,560
		7,396

What is the amount that would appear in the aged receivables analysis as owing between 0 – 30 days?

£1,667	☐
£2,279	☐
£3,450	☐
£3,119	☐

BPP
LEARNING MEDIA

Task 5.19

When analysing receivables balances it is generally believed that 80% of the value of receivables is owed by just 20% of the credit customers.

What is this rule known as?

80% rule ☐

20% rule ☐

80/20 rule ☐

20/80 rule ☐

Task 5.20

It is important to distinguish between a doubtful debt and an irrecoverable debt.

Consider the following statements:

(i) A doubtful debt will never be received and does not appear in the statement of financial position.

(ii) A doubtful debt may be received but does not appear in the statement of financial position.

Which of the statements are true?

(i) only ☐

(ii) only ☐

Both statements ☐

Neither statement ☐

BPP
LEARNING MEDIA

Task 5.21

Which of the following would be typical entries into a receivables' ledger account for a credit customer?

(i)   Invoices sent out

(ii) Statement balances sent out

(iii) Payments received

(iv) Order totals received

(i) and (ii)   ☐

(i) and (iii)   ☐

(ii) and (iii)   ☐

(iii) and (iv)   ☐

Task 5.22

A customer places an order for £5,000 which means that the balance on the customer's receivables' ledger will be £15,000 whereas the credit limit for this customer is £12,000.

What action would be required?

Despatch the goods to the customer   ☐

Put a stop on the customer's account   ☐

Discuss the situation with the customer   ☐

Make an allowance for a doubtful debt   ☐

BPP
LEARNING MEDIA

Task 5.23

A customer's outstanding balance at 30 June 20X9 has been analysed as follows:

19/04/X9	Invoice 17563	2,610
23/05/X9	Invoice 17772	1,667
01/06/X9	Credit note 4612	(331)
10/06/X9	Invoice 17890	1,890
21/06/X9	Invoice 17999	1,560
		7,396

What is the amount that would appear in the aged receivables' analysis as owing between 61 and 90 days?

£1,667 ☐

£4,277 ☐

£2,610 ☐

£3,119 ☐

Task 5.24

Analysing the aged receivables' listing should give an indication about a number of factors about a credit customer.

Which of the following could not be determined from an analysis of the aged receivables listing?

Credit limit exceeded ☐

Slow payers ☐

Customer in liquidation ☐

Old amounts outstanding but recent debts cleared ☐

Task 5.25

Which of the following would be classified as an irrecoverable debt?

An amount owing from a customer over which there is a dispute which is being discussed with the customer. ☐

An amount owing from a customer over which there is a dispute and legal proceedings have been instigated. ☐

An amount owing from a customer who has not answered the telephone, replied to letters and is no longer at their trading address. ☐

An amount owing from a customer who has gone into liquidation. ☐

Answer bank

Answer bank

Chapter 1

Task 1.1

The correct answer is: Payment of expenses using a company credit card

A credit card payment is a form of cash payment.

Task 1.2

The correct answer is: (i) and (iv)

Task 1.3

The correct answer is: Issuing an invoice to customer

Task 1.4

The correct answer is: Net 60 days 2% discount for payment within 14 days

Task 1.5

The correct answer is: The despatch of goods

Task 1.6

The correct answer is: Customer visit

Task 1.7

The correct answer is: Non-current assets

Task 1.8

The correct answer is: Ordering cycle and collection cycle

Task 1.9

The correct answer is: The ability to pay amounts when they are due

---

Task 1.10

The correct answer is: (i), (iv), (v) and (vi)

Bank references, credit agency references, trade references and recent financial statements would all be useful for assessing the credit status of a potential customer.

Task 1.11

The correct answer is: Purchase of a non-current asset in three equal instalments

---

Task 1.12

The correct answer is: Establishing customer credit status is part of the ordering cycle.

Task 1.13

The correct answer is: Net 30 days 2 % discount for 10 days

Task 1.14

The correct answer is: (ii), (iii), (iv) and (vi)

Chapter 2

Task 2.1

The correct answer is: Aged receivables' analysis

This is used for an established customer not assessing a new customer.

....

Task 2.2

The correct answer is: Bank reference, Companies House, credit reference agency

....

Task 2.3

The correct answer is: All of the above

....

Task 2.4

Gross profit margin	25%
Operating profit margin	12%
Return on capital employed	10%
Net asset turnover	0.83 times

Workings

(a) Gross profit margin = 125/500 × 100 = 25%
(b) Operating profit margin = 60/500 × 100 = 12%
(c) Return on capital employed = 60/600 × 100 = 10%
(d) Net asset turnover = 500/600 = 0.83 times

....

Task 2.5

Current ratio	1.9 : 1
Quick ratio	1.2 : 1
Inventory holding period	58 days
Accounts receivable collection period	58 days
Accounts payable payment period	73 days
Return on capital employed	5.4%
Gearing ratio	38%
Interest cover	1.75 times

Workings

(a) Current ratio = 210/108 = 1.9 : 1
(b) Quick ratio = 130/108 = 1.2 : 1
(c) Inventory holding period = (80/500) × 365 = 58 days
(d) Accounts receivable collection period = (120/750) × 365 = 58 days
(e) Accounts payable payment period = (100/500) × 365 = 73 days
(f) Return on capital employed = ((250 − 180)/(802 + 500)) × 100 = 5.4%
(g) Gearing ratio = (500/(802 + 500)) × 100 = 38%
(h) Interest cover = (250 − 180)/40 = 1.75 times

BPP LEARNING MEDIA

Task 2.6

MEMO

To: Finance Director

From: Credit Controller

Date: X-X-20X8

Subject: Request for credit from Faverly Ltd

After the request from Faverly Ltd for £20,000 of credit I have examined the information that we have available about the company which includes a bank reference, two trade references and the financial statements for the last two years.

Bank reference

The bank reference is reasonable but not as positive as it might be.

Trade references

Both trade referees note that Faverly Ltd is an occasional late payer and one of the referees did in fact suspend credit with the company for six months in 20X6. It is interesting to note that both referees only allow Faverly Ltd credit of £10,000 on 30 days credit terms.

Financial statements

The financial statements for Faverly Ltd for the last two years have been examined and the following key ratios calculated under the headings of profitability, liquidity and gearing.

	20X8	20X7
Profitability		
Gross profit margin	22%	21%
Net profit margin	12.5%	12%
Return on capital employed	11.1%	10.5%
Liquidity		
Current ratio	0.54 : 1	0.67: 1
Quick ratio	0.3 : 1	0.4 : 1
Inventory holding period	52 days	45 days
Accounts receivable collection period	51 days	58 days
Accounts payable payment period	75 days	78 days
Gearing		
Interest cover	4.3 times	5.6 times

Although the company appears to be profitable and indeed to be increasing its profitability levels there has to be considerable concern about the company's liquidity. Both the current and quick ratios are seemingly very low and are decreasing. While the company has no long-term debt it has been financed for the last two years by a substantial overdraft although the interest cover is still quite healthy at over four times.

Concern should also be raised about the accounts payable payment period which although slightly improved is still long at 75 days and considerably longer than the company's accounts receivable collection period of 51 days.

Conclusion

In the absence of any further information I suggest that we offer Faverly Ltd a trial period of credit for £10,000 on strictly 30-day terms. If these terms are not adhered to strictly then we must trade on a cash basis only with the company.

Task 2.7

Finance director

Fisher Ltd

Date:

Dear Sir

Re: Request for credit facilities

Thank you for your enquiry regarding the provision of credit facilities of £15,000 on 30-day terms. We have taken up your trade references and examined your latest set of financial statements.

We are concerned about your levels of profitability, gearing and liquidity in the most recent year and also have some concerns about one of the trade references from Froggett & Sons.

On balance we are not in a position to grant your request for trade credit at the current time although we would, of course, be delighted to trade with you on a cash basis. If you do not wish to trade on this basis and would like to enquire about credit terms in the future then we would be delighted to examine your current year's financial statements when they are available and take up an alternative trade reference.

Thank you for your interest shown in our business.

Yours faithfully

Credit controller

Task 2.8

The correct answer is: (i), (iii) and (iv)

Task 2.9

The correct answer is: Statement (i) – False, Statement (ii) True

BPP
LEARNING MEDIA

Task 2.10

To: Financial Controller

From: Assistant Accountant

Date: 17 January 20X8

Subject: Request for credit by Whittle Ltd

I have reviewed Whittle Ltd's financial statements and the references that we have received.

Ratio analysis

	This year	Last year
Current ratio	$\dfrac{1,090}{970} = 1.12$	$\dfrac{1,025}{958} = 1.07$
Acid test ratio	$\dfrac{890}{970} = 0.92$	$\dfrac{855}{958} = 0.89$
Gearing ratio	$\dfrac{500}{2,010} = 25\%$	$\dfrac{400}{1,517} = 26\%$

Current ratio

The current ratio is above 1, which means that **current assets** more than **cover current liabilities**. The current ratio has also risen since last year. The one reservation is that the rise has been due to an increase in inventory and receivables and cash has fallen slightly, indicating that control over working capital may be less efficient than in the previous year.

Quick ratio/Acid test ratio

As with the current ratio, the quick ratio has risen slightly during the year. Excluding inventory, **current assets nearly cover current liabilities** should these need to be paid.

Gearing ratio

Equity has remained at about three times long-term loan capital indicating that Whittle Ltd is **reasonably geared**. The gearing ratio has only fallen slightly this year despite extra borrowings (non-current liabilities) of £100,000, indicating that Whittle Ltd should be able to afford the extra debt.

References

The reference from **Greatlygrow Ltd** does not indicate any problems. However, Whittle Ltd has only been trading with Greatlygrow Ltd for one year, a reasonably successful one for Whittle Ltd.

Whittle Ltd has had a **much longer trading relationship**, five years, with **Weston Ltd**. However, the reference indicates that credit was suspended two years ago for six months, Despite the past problems Weston is giving Whittle Ltd two months' credit.

Recommendations

Before a final decision is taken about whether to grant credit to Whittle Ltd, **clarification of the reasons for the suspension of credit should be obtained**, and also whether there have been any other **breaches of credit terms**. A further reference, either from another long-term supplier or Whittle Ltd's bank needs to be obtained.

If the explanations and further reference is satisfactory, I recommend credit should be extended to Whittle Ltd. The credit period should initially be one month, and the account should be **closely monitored**. A **financial limit** should also be set; but you will want to consider the **size of the limit** and what should happen if the **value of the order exceeds** the desirable limit.

Task 2.11

(a) To: Financial Controller

   From: Accounting Technician

   Date:

   Subject: Request for credit facilities

We have received an application from David Jones, Financial Controller of Dreams Ltd, for credit of £20,000 on 60-day terms. However, I have the following reservations about this request.

- Dreams Ltd has **only supplied the statement of profit or loss**, not the Statement of Financial Position, restricting the financial analysis we can carry out.

- The financial statements are now **over six months old**.

- **Gross profit** and **gross profit margin** have **fallen slightly** between 20X7 and 20X8.

- The company made a **loss after tax** in 20X7 and only a small profit in 20X8.

- The terms given by the two suppliers who have provided references are stricter than the terms that Dreams Ltd has requested, £10,000 for 30 days in one case, £2,500 for 30 days in the other.

- Dreams Ltd has **not kept** to the **terms** set by Carpet Ltd, and has been taking on average 60 days to settle its account with Carpet Ltd.

- Wardrobes Ltd has **only traded** with Dreams Ltd for **three months**, and thus the assurance given by its reference is limited.

Appendix – Ratios

	20X8	*20X7*
Gross profit margin	$\dfrac{550}{1,800} \times 100\% = 30.6\%$	$\dfrac{560}{1,750} \times 100\% = 32.0\%$

(b)

> Sleepy Ltd
> Tregarn Trading Estate
> Cardiff
> CF1 3EW

Mr D. Jones
Finance Director
Dreams Ltd
17 High Street
Newport
South Wales

Date:

Dear Mr Jones

Request for credit facilities

Thank you for your application for opening credit facilities. We are pleased that you are interested in doing business with our company.

We have considered your application against our prescribed credit criteria. At present we do not feel able to offer you the facilities you request, but may be able to offer a facility of £10,000 credit on 30 days terms. In order to be able to decide whether to offer this facility, we shall need to see copies of your Statement of Financial Position from the year ended 30 June 20X8 and your most recent management accounts.

We look forward to hearing from you, and hope that we shall soon be trading with you.

Yours sincerely

....

Task 2.12

The correct answer is: Cash is going out of the business more quickly than it is coming in

If receivables are taking longer to pay money into the business than the business is taking to pay its payables then money is going out quicker than it is coming in.

....

Task 2.13

The correct answer is: (i) and (ii) only

- -

Task 2.14

The correct answer is: Do you think this customer has a good reputation?

It would not be appropriate to ask another business to make such a judgement.

- -

Task 2.15

The correct answer is: 16.0%

(£149,000 / (£400,000 + £380,000 + £150,000)) × 100 = 16.0%

- -

Task 2.16

The correct answer is: They are not audited.

- -

Task 2.17

The correct answer is: The figure gives a closer approximation to cash flow

- -

Task 2.18

The correct answer is: Details of supplier references

- -

BPP
LEARNING MEDIA

Chapter 3

Task 3.1

The correct answer is: Intention to create legal relations, consideration, agreement

Task 3.2

The correct answer is: Offer

Task 3.3

The correct answer is: (i), (iii) and (iv)

Task 3.4

The correct answer is: Condition

Task 3.5

The correct answer is: Action for the price

Task 3.6

The correct answer is: County Court

Task 3.7

The correct answer is: A court bailiff seizes and sells the receivable's goods on behalf of the business

Task 3.8

The correct answer is: A demand for payment from an outstanding receivable of £750 or more

Task 3.9

The correct answer is: Secured creditors, bankruptcy costs, preferential creditors, unsecured creditors

Task 3.10

The correct answer is: Unsecured creditors

Task 3.11

The correct answer is: Bankruptcy

Bankruptcy relates to individuals, not to companies.

Task 3.12

The correct answer is: An individual whose data is held

Task 3.13

The correct answer is: They do what they are expected to do.

Task 3.14

The correct answer is: Gross Debt × (base rate + 8%) × (No. of days overdue/365)

Task 3.15

The correct answer is: Slow track

BPP
LEARNING MEDIA

Task 3.16

The correct answer is: Neither (i) nor (ii) is correct

....

Task 3.17

The correct answer is: (ii) only

Consideration need only be sufficient – it need not be adequate.

....

Task 3.18

The correct answer is: An auction bid

The others are invitations to treat.

....

Task 3.19

The correct answer is: (i), (ii) and (iv)

Offer and acceptance, consideration and intention to create legal relations are essential requirements of a contract.

....

Task 3.20

The correct answer is: Express terms

....

Task 3.21

The correct answer is: 8

....

Task 3.22

The correct answer is: No. Brian's letter has varied the terms and so is a counter-offer, rejecting Alexander's original offer.

Brian varied the terms of the offer when replying to Alexander.

....

Task 3.23

The correct answer is: (ii) only

Task 3.24

The correct answer is: The promise of an exchange of value

BPP
LEARNING MEDIA

Chapter 4

Task 4.1

The correct answer is 7.4%

$$\text{Cost of discount} = \frac{d}{100-d} \times \frac{365}{N-D}$$

where d = discount percentage given

N = normal payment term

D = discount payment term

$$\text{Cost of discount} \frac{1}{100-1} \times \frac{365}{60-10} = 7.4\%$$

....

Task 4.2

The correct answer is: Cost = 18.8%, Introduce or not = No.

$$\text{Cost of early settlement} = \frac{d}{(100-d)} \times \frac{365}{(N-D)}$$

$$= \frac{3}{(100-3)} \times \frac{365}{(60-0)}$$

$$= 18.8\%$$

As 18.8% is greater than the 15% the company uses to appraise investments, the discount is not worthwhile.

....

Task 4.3

The correct answer is: 17.7%

$$\text{Cost of discount} = \left(\frac{d}{100-d} \times \frac{365}{(N-D)} \right)\%$$

$$= \left(\frac{2.5}{100-2.5} \times \frac{365}{60-7} \right)\%$$

$$= 17.7\%$$

....

Task 4.4

The correct answer is: £240,000

The existing value of receivables is: $\dfrac{£18m}{12 \text{ months}}$ = £1.5m

If sales increased by 60,000 units, the value of receivables would be:

$2 \times \dfrac{£18m + (60,000 \times £10)}{12 \text{ months}}$ = £3.1 million

The receivables have to be financed somehow, and the additional £1.6 million will cost £1,600,000 × 15% = £240,000 in financing costs.

Task 4.5

The correct answer is: Despatch of goods

Task 4.6

The correct answer is: (ii) only

The amounts advanced by the invoice discounter are at a discount to the carrying amount (book value) of the receivables.

Task 4.7

The correct answer is: A business lends money to a customer based on a discounted value of the invoices that customer has issued

Task 4.8

The correct answer is: Claim back amounts owed to it by customers who have defaulted

Task 4.9

The correct answer is: Whole turnover policy

BPP
LEARNING MEDIA

Task 4.10

The correct answer is: Statement (i) and statement (ii) are both false.

Statement (i) describes a credit reference agency. Statement (ii) describes the services of a factor. A credit collection agency specialises in the collection of debts that are proving difficult to obtain in the normal course of business.

Task 4.11

The correct answer is: Neither statement is true

Task 4.12

The correct answer is:

$$\text{Cost of discount} = \frac{1.5}{100 - 1.5} \times \frac{365}{30 - 14} \times 100$$

$$= 34.7\%$$

Not worthwhile as the cost of bank interest is only 6%.

Task 4.13

The correct answer is: A percentage of amounts collected

Task 4.14

The correct answer is: (ii), (iii) and (v)

Overdraft interest should be saved as the money is received from the factor earlier than the receivables would have paid. As the money is received earlier, it should be possible to pay suppliers earlier, avoiding interest from suppliers or late payment penalties.

Task 4.15

The correct answer is: Re-instigating receivables ledger

Task 4.16

The correct answer is: About 80% of receivables are covered for their entire amount.

Task 4.17

The correct answer is: £1,000 loss

Working

New receivables	=	£390,000 × 2/12
	=	£65,000
Increase in receivables	=	£40,000
Increase in profit	=	£390,000 × 10%
	=	£39,000
Overall loss	=	£1,000

Task 4.18

The correct answer is: 24.5%

Working

$$\text{Cost of discount} = \frac{3}{100-3} \times \frac{365}{60-14} \times 100$$

$$= 24.5\%$$

Task 4.19

The correct answer is: (ii), (iv) and (v)

Task 4.20

The correct answer is: (i) only

BPP
LEARNING MEDIA

Chapter 5

Task 5.1

The correct answer is: The maximum amount allowed to be outstanding at any point in time

Task 5.2

	Total £	Credit limit £	Current, < 30 days £	31 – 60 days £	61 – 90 days £	> 90 days £
Knightly Ltd	24,519	30,000	11,333	8,448	4,738	

Task 5.3

Jeremy Ltd There is one long outstanding amount of £890 which would appear to be a problem. The customer's file should be checked to see if there is any correspondence about this amount and if not a telephone call should be made to the customer to determine the problem with the payment. Consideration might be given to providing an allowance for this amount as a doubtful debt.

Lenter Ltd This receivable would appear to be a consistent slow payer as the amounts are equally stretched over the current period up to 90 days. The customer should be consulted about its slow payment record and incentives for earlier payment such as settlement discounts offered.

Friday Partners This amount is of great concern as not only has it been outstanding for more than 61 days but there is no current trading with the customer. The customer should be contacted urgently in order to determine any problem with the payment of the debt.

Diamond & Co This customer appears to be a slightly slow payer but of more importance is that their credit limit has been exceeded by over £1,000. The reason for this exceeding of the credit limit should be investigated and if necessary no further sales to this customer should be made until the earlier invoices are paid.

Task 5.4

MEMORANDUM

To: Sales Manager

From: Credit Controller

Date: 6 December

Subject: Aged receivables' analysis

Megacorp plc

32% of this major customer's debt is over 90 days old. Although clearly a key customer, Megacorp plc appears to be taking unfair advantage of its 60 days net credit terms.

For the future, we should consider:

(a) Offering a discount for early payment

(b) Improving communication with Megacorp plc's payables ledger department and senior management to help ensure prompt payment

(c) Sending prompt reminder letters, followed-up by telephone calls

(d) Reviewing the credit limit for the company

Goodfellows Cycles Ltd

Goodfellows Cycles Ltd appears generally to be a prompt payer within the 30 days terms set for the customer. However, a debt of £5,000 is currently outstanding for over 90 days.

I recommend that:

(a) The £5,000 debt outstanding for over 90 days should be investigated to check whether there is some dispute. Perhaps a relatively minor query is holding up payment.

(b) We should consider ways of increasing sales to the customer.

(c) Procedures for dealing with customer queries should be reviewed.

Hooper-bikes Ltd

Hooper-bikes has a total amount outstanding in excess of its credit limit. 60 days' credit is allowed to this customer, but 40% of its debt is overdue. This is not a satisfactory situation, and urgent action should be taken.

For the future, I recommend that:

(a) The credit limit for the customer should be reviewed.

(b) We make sure that the debt outstanding is brought to within the current credit limit as soon as possible.

(c) We consider how to improve this customer's payment record, perhaps by insisting on cash with order.

(d) We review order procedures to avoid customers being supplied with goods which take their account beyond its credit limit.

Dynamo Cycles Ltd

There are no current problems regarding this smaller customer's account. Credit taken up is within the credit limit and no debt is overdue.

For the future we might:

(a) Try to increase sales to Dynamo
(b) Review this customer's credit limit

Task 5.5

Carnford Ltd – The amount is more than 60 days overdue and a visit to the customer might be in order to see if we can obtain payment without resort to legal proceedings. If a visit is not successful then legal proceedings should be considered subject to the agreement of the finance director. As the amount is large and over 60 days overdue, an allowance should be made for the entire amount.

Luxford Ltd – A telephone call should be made to remind the company that there is a balance of £900 overdue and, in particular, to discover the reason for the amount of £180 that has been overdue for more than 60 days. No allowance is necessary as yet.

KLP Ltd – All of the amount outstanding is overdue and £960 is at least 30 days overdue. The customer should be considered being placed on the stop list and a meeting arranged to clarify the position.

Flanders Ltd – This appears to be a consistent customer but of the total overdue amount of £8,210, £1,985 is more than 30 days overdue. A reminder letter and telephone call should be made to the customer and consideration should be given to putting the customer on the stop list. However, as this seems to be regular customer this should only be done after serious consideration especially if other negotiations will suffice.

Task 5.6

Finance Controller

Harvey Ltd

Date:

Dear Sir

Account No: 204764

I do not appear to have received payment of the amount of £1,350.46 which is 14 days overdue. I trust that this is an oversight and that you will arrange for immediate payment to be made. If you are withholding payment for any reason, please contact me urgently and I will be pleased to assist you.

If you have already made payment please advise me and accept my apology for having troubled you.

Yours faithfully

Credit controller

Task 5.7

Financial Controller

Bart & Sons

Date

Dear Sir

Account No: B245

I do not appear to have received payment of the amount of £976.80 which is now 30 days overdue. I trust that this is an oversight and that you will arrange for immediate payment to be made. If you are withholding payment for any reason, please contact me urgently and I will be pleased to assist you.

I regret that unless payment is received within the next seven days I will have no alternative but to stop any further sales on credit to you until the amount owing is cleared in full. If you have already made payment please advise me and accept my apology for having troubled you.

Yours faithfully

Credit Controller

Task 5.8

The correct answer is: If 20% of the largest customers are analysed this should account for 80% in value.

Task 5.9

Manton Ltd Aged Receivables' Analysis – 31 October 20X7

Customer name and ref	Total amount	Current < 1 month	Outstanding 1-2 months	Outstanding 2-3 months	Outstanding >3 months
New Milton	£13,000	£4,000 M98	£2,000 M89		£7,000 M17
Sway	£1,000		£1,000 M81		
Mudeford	£0				
Barton	£17,000	£4,000 M101		£13,000 M69	
Boscombe	£5,000	£5,000 M103			
TOTAL	**£36,000**	**£13,000**	**£3,000**	**£13,000**	**£7,000**

BPP LEARNING MEDIA

Task 5.10

The correct answer is: Largest debts should be pursued as a first priority with smallest amounts pursued last.

Task 5.11

The correct answer is: Telephone Jines Ltd to enquire about the situation in order to determine whether there is any query regarding the amount outstanding and to agree steps for payment.

Task 5.12

The correct answer is: £4,277

These are the April and May outstanding amounts.

Task 5.13

The correct answer is: An irrecoverable debt is written off and does not appear in the statement of financial position.

Task 5.14

The correct answer is: Inventory ordering

Inventory ordering would not be part of an organisation's credit control policy.

Task 5.15

The correct answer is: (i), (ii) and (v)

Task 5.16

The correct answer is: At any point in time the customer's balance must not exceed £10,000.

Task 5.17

The correct answer is: It could result in an irrecoverable debt.

Task 5.18

The correct answer is: £3,119

£1,890 + £1,560 – £331

Task 5.19

The correct answer is: 80/20 rule

Task 5.20

The correct answer is: Neither statement

A doubtful debt may not be received but an allowance is made against it rather than removing it from the statement of financial position.

Task 5.21

The correct answer is: (i) and (iii)

Task 5.22

The correct answer is: Discuss the situation with the customer

---

Task 5.23

The correct answer is: £2,610

BPP
LEARNING MEDIA

Task 5.24

The correct answer is: Customer in liquidation

....

Task 5.25

The correct answer is: An amount owing from a customer who has not answered the telephone, replied to letters and is no longer at their trading address

If there are discussions or legal proceedings including administration then there is a likelihood of the debt being recovered. However, if the customer no longer appears to exist then this is more than likely to be an irrecoverable debt.

....

BPP
LEARNING MEDIA

AAT AQ2013 SAMPLE ASSESSMENT
CREDIT CONTROL

Time allowed: 2 hours 30 minutes

AAT AQ2013
SAMPLE ASSESSMENT

BPP
LEARNING MEDIA

Task 1 (20 marks)

(a) **Consideration must be**:

Of economic value ☐

Of some value, even if it is minimal value ☐

A cash amount ☐

A cash amount which can be easily converted to cash ☐

(b) **The essential features of a simple contract include**:

Offer, acceptance, market value and written terms ☐

Invitation to treat, offer, acceptance and written terms ☐

Offer, acceptance, the exchange of value and intention to create legal relations ☐

Offer, invitation to accept, consideration and a signature ☐

(c) **Which one of the following is a key term of the Sale of Goods Act?**

Goods must be of "satisfactory quality". ☐

Goods must be "the best available quality". ☐

Goods must be "durable quality". ☐

Goods must be "top quality". ☐

Bert is the owner of a furniture shop. He places a notice in the window advertising the sale of sofas at half price.

(d) **The notice is:**

A unilateral offer ☐

An invitation to treat ☐

An acceptance of an offer ☐

A contractual offer ☐

Barry orders goods from Mary by sending her a purchase order (PO). Mary confirmed the order by sending a contract in writing stating that the terms include a requirement that Barry notify Mary of any damaged goods within 48 hours. Barry signed the contract and returned it to Mary.

(e) **Select the correct answer from the list below.**

[▼]

Picklist:

The PO sent by Barry is an invitation to treat and Mary's contract is an offer.

The PO sent by Barry is an offer and Mary's contract is a counter offer

(f) **Which of the following is correct?**

Misrepresentation is the basic remedy for a breach of contract. ☐

Specific performance is the common remedy for breach of contract. ☐

Damages is the basic remedy available for a breach of contract. ☐

Specific injunction is the common remedy for breach of contract. ☐

The Late Payment of Commercial Debts (Interest) Act allows small companies to charge interest to customers who pay late. The rate of interest is set by statute and by reference to the Bank of England base rate.

(g) **If the current base rate is 2.5% the late payment interest rate is** [   ] **%.**

A customer owes £3,000 excluding VAT and the debt is 45 days late. The current Bank of England base rate is 1.5%. Calculate the interest charge under the Late Payments of Commercial Debts (Interest) Act to the nearest penny.

(h) **The interest charge will be £** ☐ .

The Data Protection Act states that anyone who processes personal information must comply with eight principles.

(i) **Which THREE of the following are principles contained in the Data Protection Act?**

Fairly and unlawfully processed ☐

Any data about an individual ☐

Processed for limited purposes ☐

Adequate, relevant, excessive and appropriate ☐

Not kept for longer than 24 months ☐

Applies to manual and computer records ☐

Task 2 (20 marks)

(a) **Which one of the following is correct for an Administrative Receivership?**

The Administrator is an insolvency practitioner appointed by the company to deal with the affairs of the insolvent company. The principal role of the Administrative Receiver is to secure the best outcome for his appointer albeit retaining a limited duty of care to the remaining creditors of the company. ☐

Administrative Receivership is the appointment of an insolvency practitioner by a creditor who holds a fixed charge over the assets of the company. The principal role of the Administrative Receiver is to secure the best outcome for his appointer albeit retaining a limited duty of care to the remaining creditors of the company. ☐

Administrative Receivership is the appointment of an insolvency practitioner by a creditor who holds a floating charge over the assets of the company. The principal role of the Administrative Receiver is to secure the best outcome for his appointer albeit retaining a limited duty of care to the remaining creditors of the company. ☐

Administrative Receivership is a process requiring a licensed insolvency practitioner to act as the Administrator appointed by the court. The court appointed Administrator takes over the management of the company and takes responsibility for restructuring the company or business. ☐

A sole trader is having difficulty obtaining payment from a customer who is also a sole trader.

This is a breach of contract.

(b) **Which type of remedy can the sole trader pursue?**

An action for specific performance ☐

An administration order ☐

A winding up order ☐

An action for price ☐

(c) **What is a warrant of execution?**

A court order requesting that a company make payment directly to the creditor. ☐

A court order authorising bailiffs to enter business premises and seize goods which will then be sold to settle a debt. ☐

A court order authorising liquidators to recover property under a retention of title clause and return the property to the creditor. ☐

A court order authorising creditors to enter business premises and seize goods which will then be sold to settle a debt. ☐

(d) **Retention of title will normally be valid if**:

The contract contains a retention of title clause and the goods have been delivered. ☐

The goods cannot be identified and have been converted. ☐

The retention of title clause has been included in the contract and the goods are identifiable. ☐

The goods have been bolted onto a larger piece of equipment and therefore are now part of the new equipment. ☐

(e) **In order to petition the court for a winding up order, the creditor must be owed**:

At least £750 ☐

At least £7,500 ☐

At least £750 but less than £75,000 ☐

Between £75 and £750 ☐

Wilko has been trading with Jonny for many years. Jonny purchased 1,200,000 units of goods in 20X3. The sales price of the product is £6 per unit including VAT. At the 31 December 20X3 Jonny owed Wilko £986,301.

(f) **The receivable collection period in days for the amount owing by Jonny is [   ] days.**

(g) **Which TWO of the following could be used to assess the credit status of a new customer?**

Aged trade receivables analysis ☐

Management accounts ☐

Trading history ☐

Copies of purchase orders ☐

A company's terms of payment are 45 days. It is offering a discount of 2% for payment within 7 days.

(h) **The simple annual interest rate of the discount is [   ] %.**

ABC Limited is looking to improve its cash flow and has been considering various finance products. ABC has a balance on its sales ledger of £1,254,356 as at the 30 June 20X3.

A finance company has offered to provide a facility where ABC can borrow up to £900,000 or a maximum of 75% of the total outstanding sales ledger balance. The finance company administers the sales ledger on behalf of ABC for a fee of £2,000 per month.

(i) **Complete the following sentence**.

The maximum amount available to borrow at the 30 June 20X3 is [   ]

and the product is [▼]

Picklist:

An invoice discounting facility.
A factoring facility.
A term bank loan.
A mortgage loan.

Task 3 (24 marks)

You work as a Credit Control Manager for Apollo Limited which uses a credit rating system to assess the credit status of new customers. The credit rating (scoring) system below is used to assess the risk of default by calculating key indicators (ratios), comparing them to the table and calculating an aggregate score.

Credit rating (scoring) system	Score
Operating profit margin	
Losses	-5
Less than 5%	0
5% and above but less than 10%	5
10% and above but less than 20%	10
20% or more	20
Interest cover	
No cover	-30
Less than 1	-20
1 and above but less than 2	-10
2 and above but less than 4	0
4 or more	10

Credit rating (scoring) system	Score
Liquidity ratio	
Less than 1	-20
1 and above but less than 1.25	-10
1.25 and above but less than 1.5	0
1.5 or more	10
Gearing (total debt/total debt plus equity)	
Less than 25%	20
25% and above but less than 50%	10
50% and above but less than 65%	0
65% and above but less than 75%	-20
75% and above but less than 80%	-40
80% or more	-100

Risk	Aggregate score
Very low risk	Between 60 and 21
Low risk	Between 20 and 1
Medium risk	Between 0 and -24
High risk	Between -25 and -50
Very high risk	Between -50 and -160

The sales department has asked for a credit limit of £56,000 to be given to X Limited who is a potential new customer. The financial information below has been supplied by X Limited.

X Limited Statement of profit or loss	20X2	20X1
	£'000	£'000
Sales revenue	3,900	3,200
Cost of sales	3,204	2,445
Gross profit	**696**	**755**
Distribution costs	450	600
Administration expenses	480	315
Operating profit	**(234)**	**(160)**
Finance costs	190	170
Profit before taxation	**(424)**	**(330)**
Taxation	0	0
Profit for the year	**(424)**	**(330)**

X Limited Statement of Financial Position	20X2	20X1
	£'000	£'000
ASSETS		
Non-current assets		
Property, plant and equipment	4,906	5,565
Current assets		
Inventories	690	650
Trade and other receivables	860	800
Cash	190	455
	1,740	1,905
Total assets	**6,646**	**7,470**
EQUITY AND LIABILITIES		
Equity		
Share capital	100	100
Retained earnings	176	600
Total equity	**276**	**700**
Non-current liabilities		
Borrowing	5,500	5,500
Current liabilities		
Borrowings	400	800
Trade and other payables	470	470
Total liabilities	**6,370**	**6,770**
Total equity and liabilities	**6,646**	**7,470**

(a) **Complete the table below by calculating the key indicators (to 2 decimal places) for 20X2 and 20X1 for X Limited, and rate the company using the credit rating scoring system.**

X Limited	20X2 Indicator	20X2 Rating	20X1 Indicator	20X1 Rating
Operating profit margin %				
Interest cover				
Current ratio				
Gearing %				
Total credit rating				

Rating	Decision
Very low or low risk current year and very low or low risk previous year	Accept
Very low or low risk current year and medium risk previous year	Accept
Very low or low risk current year and high or very high risk previous year	Request latest management accounts and defer decision
Very high risk or high risk current year	Reject
Medium risk current year and medium, low or very low risk previous year	Accept
Medium risk current year and high or very high risk previous year	Request latest management accounts and defer decision

(b) **Based on the results of your credit rating and using the table above, recommend whether the requested credit limit should be given to X Limited.**

Customer	Decision
X Limited	▼

Picklist:

Accept
Reject
Request latest management accounts and defer decision

BPP LEARNING MEDIA

Task 4 (24 marks)

The sales department has asked for a credit limit of £45,000 to be given to Z Limited who is a potential new customer. The financial information below has been supplied by Z Limited.

Z Limited Statement of profit or loss	20X2	20X1
	£'000	£'000
Sales revenue	4,960	5,500
Cost of sales	3,700	4,210
Gross profit	**1,260**	**1,290**
Distribution costs	600	640
Administration expenses	700	700
Operating profit	**(40)**	**(50)**
Finance costs	200	160
Profit before taxation	**(240)**	**(210)**
Taxation	0	0
Profit for the year	**(240)**	**(210)**

Z Limited Statement of Financial Position	20X2	20X1
	£'000	£'000
ASSETS		
Non-current assets		
Property, plant and equipment	2,930	2,365
Current assets		
Inventories	760	810
Trade and other receivables	800	760
Cash	100	500
	1,660	2,070
Total assets	4,590	4,435
EQUITY AND LIABILITIES		
Equity		
Share capital	1,000	1,000
Retained earnings	560	800
Total equity	1,560	1,800
Non-current liabilities		
Borrowing	1,800	1,600
Current liabilities		
Trade and other payables	1,230	1,035
Total liabilities	3,030	2,635
Total equity and liabilities	4,590	4,435

(a) **Complete the table below by calculating the key indicators (to 2 decimal places) for 20X2 and 20X1 for Z Limited**.

Z Limited	20X2 Indicator	20X1 Indicator
Gross profit margin %		
Operating profit margin %		
Trade payables payment period in days		
Inventory holding period in days		
Current ratio		
Quick ratio		

(b) **Complete the email to the chief credit controller commenting on the ratios calculated in (a) above and conclude by recommending whether or not credit should be extended.**

Email

To: Credit controller

From: AAT Technician

Date: Today

Subject: New Customer Z Limited

Please find below my observations and recommendation for new customer Z Limited.

Profitability

The revenue has decreased by [   ] % which means that the company

has [▼]

The gross profit margin has increased by [   ] %. The company has

[▼]

The company is loss making at the operational level with the operating loss at £40,000 in 20X2.

[▼]

Picklist 1:

Either sold fewer units or decreased the price of its product.
Decreased sales which means the company is overtrading.
Increased its price to increase demand.

Picklist 2:

Reduced the sales price of the product to maintain demand.
Increased the sales price of the product.
Increased the price of purchasing the product.

Picklist 3:

This is not a problem as cash pays liabilities not profits.
This may be a problem depending on the cash flow of the business.
This is a problem because profits are needed to pay liabilities.
This is not a problem as gross profit is enough to pay for the liabilities.

Liquidity

The current ratio provides [▼]

In this case it has fallen and is [▼]

The inventory level has [▼]

[▼]

[▼]

The trade payables payment period in days has [▼] by [ ] days.

[▼]

I recommend that [▼]

Picklist 1:

A rough measure of the short term solvency of the organisation.
A measure of long term solvency.1
A measure of insolvency.

Picklist 2:

Still greater than 1 which is a good sign.
Less than 1 which is a sign of insolvency.
Less than 1 which is a sign of poor liquidity.

Picklist 3:

Decreased.
Increased.

Picklist 4:

This is a good sign but the holding period has increased which means inventory may be slow moving.

This is a good sign but the holding period has decreased which means inventory may run out.

This is a bad sign as inventory levels are too low.

This is a bad sign and indicates high levels of old inventory.

BPP
LEARNING MEDIA

Picklist 5:

The quick ratio has fallen below 1 which is a major concern and supports the conclusion of poor liquidity.

The quick ratio has fallen below 1 which is not a concern and supports the conclusion of good liquidity.

The quick ratio has fallen below 0 which is a major concern and supports the conclusion of poor liquidity.

The quick ratio has fallen below 1 which is a major concern and means the company is insolvent.

The quick ratio has fallen slightly but is still greater than 0 which is positive and shows liquidity.

Picklist 6:

Decreased
Increased

Picklist 7:

It appears that the company may have insufficient liquidity and is unlikely to pay its liabilities as they fall due.

It appears that the company has sufficient liquidity and is unlikely to pay its liabilities as they fall due.

The company is insolvent and cannot pay its liabilities as they fall due.

It appears that the company has sufficient liquidity and is likely to pay its liabilities as they fall due.

Picklist 8:

Credit be given.
Credit not be given.

Task 5 (24 marks)

Y Limited has been trading with Bravo Limited for several years and has, until recently, always paid to terms. Following several late payments they have now contacted Bravo Limited to request an increase in their credit limit from £100,000 to £200,000. Y Limited has supplied the accounts below:

Y Limited Statement of profit or loss	20X2	20X1
	£'000	£'000
Sales revenue	11,700	6,500
Cost of sales	8,100	4,300
Gross profit	**3,600**	**2,200**
Distribution costs	1,650	1,230
Administration expenses	500	500
Operating profit	**1,450**	**470**
Finance costs	300	200
Profit before taxation	**1,150**	**270**
Taxation	400	70
Profit for the year	**750**	**200**

Y Limited Statement of Financial Position	20X2	20X1
	£'000	£'000
ASSETS		
Non-current assets		
Property, plant and equipment	2,150	2,400
Current assets		
Inventories	1,400	800
Trade and other receivables	2,400	1,200
Cash	600	0
	4,400	2,000
Total assets	**6,550**	**4,400**

BPP
LEARNING MEDIA

EQUITY AND LIABILITIES		
Equity		
Share capital	200	100
Retained earnings	1,250	500
Total equity	**1,450**	**600**
Non-current liabilities		
Borrowing	4,000	1,800
Current liabilities		
Bank overdraft	0	1,200
Trade and other payables	1,100	800
Total liabilities	**5,100**	**3,800**
Total equity and liabilities	**6,550**	**4,400**

Y Limited	20X2	20X1
Gross profit margin %	30.77	33.85
Operating profit margin %	12.39	7.23
Interest cover	4.83	2.35
Current ratio	4.00	1.00
Trade payables payment period in days	50	68
Trade receivables collection period in days	75	67
Inventory holding period in days	63	68
Gearing %	73.39	83.33

The sales manager has reviewed the information provided by Y Limited and has made the following comments:

I think that the company is a good risk because of the following factors:

1. The company turnover has increased by 44% from £6.5 million to £11.7 million. This is a strong sign of overtrading.

2. The operating profit has increased from £470,000 to £1,450,000. This means that more cash is available to pay debts.

3. The interest cover has increased from 2.35 times to 4.83 times which means that the company is in a worse position than last year.

4. The current ratio should be 2 which means that last year the company was insolvent, but this year the company is solvent.

5. The trade receivables has increased by £1,200,000 which supports the conclusion of overtrading.

6.   The trade payables are down from 68 days to 50 days implying that the company is struggling to get credit from its suppliers.

7.   The inventory has increased by £600,000 which supports the conclusion of overtrading.

8.   Gearing has decreased which means that the banks are not happy to lend money to the business.

9.   My conclusion is that credit should not be given.

Write a brief note dealing with each comment that the sales manager has made. Explain any other indicator which aids the conclusion you make as to whether credit should be given.

BPP
LEARNING MEDIA

Task 6 (18 marks)

You have been provided with the credit control policy for Alpha Ltd. Today's date is 30 September 20X3.

Current credit control procedures once credit limit has been agreed:

1. An order for goods is received by email, fax or phone (all phone calls are recorded).

2. Goods are delivered and a goods received note is signed by the customer.

3. The goods received notes are kept in a file in the accounts office.

4. An invoice will be issued on the day after delivery on 30 day terms.

5. An aged analysis of trade receivables is produced weekly.

6. A reminder telephone call is made when the debt is 7 days overdue.

7. When a debt is 14 days overdue a letter is sent.

8. When the debt is 28 days overdue the account will be put on stop.

9. The debt will either be placed in the hands of a debt collection company or legal proceedings could be instigated if the customer does not respond to calls or letters.

10. The business is credit insured, however insurance is only given for customers once they have a history of trade with the business of at least 12 months and have successfully paid for at least 3 invoiced amounts. Only 80% of the value of the debt is insured. VAT will be reclaimed from HMRC.

The assistant responsible for credit control has been on sick leave for several months but you have access to notes she prepared.

Identify the most appropriate course of action for each customer based on the information provided.

Customer A

The balance on Customer A's account is £24,500. This consists of two invoices, one for £17,250 which is not overdue and one for £7,250 which is overdue. An unallocated payment has been received for £7,250 and posted to the unallocated payment accounts in the purchase ledger. It has now been indentified as a receipt from Customer A.

The action needed is to [▼]

Picklist:

Credit customer A's account with £7,250 and debit unallocated payments with £7,250.
Debit customer A's account with £7,250 and debit unallocated payments with £7,250.
Credit customer A's account with £7,250 and credit unallocated payments with £7,250.
Debit customer A's account with £7,250 and credit unallocated payments with £7,250.

Customer B

This is a new customer who placed their first order a few weeks ago. The goods were delivered on 1 September 20X3 and the invoice was raised on 10 September 20X3 on 30 day terms.

The account should be put on stop. ☐

The account is not overdue so no action is required. ☐

The customer should be contacted and an immediate payment requested. ☐

A phone call should have been made on 17 September 20X3 and a letter sent on 24 September 20X3. ☐

Customer C

A balance of £36,250 is 64 days overdue and is for one invoice. Customer C claims that the goods were not received.

Send the original delivery note signed by Customer C. ☐

Raise a credit note for £36,250. ☐

Send a copy of the signed delivery note which was signed by Customer C. ☐

Send a copy of the signed delivery note signed by the courier who delivered the package. ☐

Customer D

Customer D sent a payment of £25,000 but did not provide details of which invoices the payment relates to.

Customer D should be contacted to confirm which invoices are being paid so that the unallocated receipt can be allocated. ☐

The £25,000 should be returned to Customer D. ☐

The £25,000 should be allocated to the last invoices first. ☐

The £25,000 should be posted to unallocated payments. ☐

Customer E

Customer E owes a balance of £55,200 including VAT. The account is on stop. Attempts to contact the customer by telephone and letter have been unsuccessful. The account is credit insured.

Complete the sentence below.

Contact the credit insurer to make a claim for: £ [   ] , make a provision for:

£ [   ] and claim VAT of £ [   ] from HMRC.

Customer F

Customer F has gone into administration after being a customer for five years. Up until six months ago, they had always paid to terms.

Place the account on stop and contact a debt collection company to deal with processing a claim against Customer F. ☐

Contact the insolvency service and register a claim with the credit insurer. ☐

Visit the premises of Customer F and seize goods to the value of the outstanding balance. ☐

Contact the insolvency practitioner and register a claim with the credit insurer. ☐

Task 7 (18 marks)

Moss Ltd supplies goods to the manufacturing sector. Each product is stamped with a batch number so that they can be easily identified. The standard terms and conditions printed on the back of every sales invoice raised by Moss Ltd include a retention of title clause and a clause that problems with goods must be notified to Moss Ltd within 24 hours of delivery. Goods returned are subject to a restocking fee of 10%.

You work in the credit control department and the date is 30 June 20X3, the company's financial year end.

The senior credit controller is ill but has left you a copy of the company's credit control policy together with notes on some of the customer accounts. An extract of these notes is provided below:

Current credit control procedures once a credit limit has been agreed:

1. An order for goods is received by email, fax or phone (all phone calls are recorded).
2. Goods are delivered and a goods received note is signed by the customer.
3. The goods received notes are kept in a file in the accounts office.
4. An invoice will be issued on the day after delivery on 30 day terms.
5. An aged analysis of trade receivables is produced weekly.
6. A reminder telephone call is made when the debt is 7 days overdue.

7. When a debt is 14 days overdue a letter is sent.

8. When the account is 28 days overdue the account will be put on stop.

9. The debt will either be placed in the hands of a debt collection company or legal proceedings could be instigated if the customer does not respond to calls or letters.

10. The business is credit insured, however insurance is only given for customers once they have a history of trade with the business of at least 12 months and have successfully paid for at least 3 invoiced amounts. Only 70% of the debt is insured.

11. All sales invoices include VAT at the standard rate of 20% and VAT is recovered from HMRC under the bad debt relief scheme where applicable.

(a) **Review the information provided for each of the three customers below and prepare an action plan for collecting the outstanding amounts due to Moss Ltd. Your action plan should include a summary of the options available for the company to pursue and recommendations for provisions or write off of irrecoverable debts where appropriate.**

Botton Ltd

The sales ledger of Moss Ltd shows a balance outstanding of £48,000 which is now 60 days overdue. The bookkeeper at Botton Ltd has said that they have a problem with their online banking system and are unable to make any payments by BACS.

Hamiltons

Hamiltons has gone into receivership owing Moss Ltd £15,000 plus VAT at 20%. Moss Ltd has contacted the receiver who has stated that it is unlikely that the retention of title will be valid because the company purchased similar items from several suppliers and therefore the goods are not identifiable as being supplied by Moss Ltd. The receiver also stated that the existing debt will be classed as an unsecured creditor of Hamiltons.

Schumaker & Co

Schumaker & Co are refusing to pay an invoice of £27,000 from May 20X3 claiming that product BP20 was ordered but product BP21 was delivered. They are requesting that Moss Ltd collect BP21 and deliver product BP20. Schumaker has been a customer for many years and is always in the top 5 for total orders and normally pays promptly.

Additional information

Hill Ltd

The sales ledger account for Hill Ltd has become corrupted but the following information is available:

Balance 1 March 20X3 – £150,000

Invoices raised:

9 March 20X3 – £50,000 plus VAT at 20%
15 April 20X3 – £80,400 (VAT inclusive)

Credit notes raised:

6 March 20X3 – £48,000 (VAT inclusive) subject to a restocking fee of 10%
20 April 20X3 – £24,000 (VAT inclusive) not subject to a restocking fee

Bank receipts:

16 March 20X3 – £150,000
16 April 20X3 – £90,000

(b) **What is the balance on the account of Hill Ltd at 31 March 20X3 and at 30 April 20X3?**

Additional information

No action has been taken in respect of the account for customer Vettel (agreed credit limit of £20,000).

The account transactions are listed below, and today's date is 30 June 20X3:

- Invoice of £26,000 plus VAT at 20% on 15 March 20X3 for a delivery made on 14 March 20X3.

- Invoice of £16,000 plus VAT at 20% on 5 May 20X3 for a delivery made on 4 May 20X3.

(c) **Identify the actions, with dates, that should have been undertaken by the credit control team at Moss Ltd for Vettel.**

BPP
LEARNING MEDIA

AAT AQ2013 SAMPLE ASSESSMENT
CREDIT CONTROL

ANSWERS

AAT AQ2013 SAMPLE ASSESSMENT
CREDIT CONTROL

ANSWERS

BPP
LEARNING MEDIA

Task 1 (20 marks)

(a) **Consideration must be:**

Of economic value ☐

Of some value, even if it is minimal value ☑

Of cash amount ☐

Of cash amount which can be easily converted to cash ☐

(b) **The essential features of a simple contract include:**

Offer, acceptance, market value and written terms ☐

Invitation to treat, offer, acceptance and written terms ☐

Offer, acceptance, the exchange of value and intention to create legal relations ☑

Offer, invitation to accept, consideration and a signature ☐

(c) **Which one of the following is a key term of the Sale of Goods Act?**

Goods must be of "satisfactory quality". ☑

Goods must be "the best available quality". ☐

Goods must be "durable quality". ☐

Goods must be "top quality" ☐

(d) **The notice is:**

A unilateral offer ☐

An invitation to treat ☑

An acceptance of an offer ☐

A contractual offer ☐

(e)

The PO sent by Barry is an offer and Mary's contract is a counter offer. ▼

(f)

Misrepresentation is the basic remedy for a breach of contract. ☐

Specific performance is the common remedy for breach of contract. ☐

Damages is the basic remedy available for breach of contract. ☑

Specific injunction is the common remedy for breach of contract. ☐

(g) **If the current base rate 2.5% the late payment interest rate is** `10.50` **%.**

(h) **The interest charge will be £** `42.16` .

(i)

Fairly and unlawfully processed ☐

Any data about an individual ☑

Processed for limited purposes ☑

Adequate, relevant, excessive and appropriate ☐

Not kept for longer than 24 months ☐

Applies to manual and computer records ☑

BPP LEARNING MEDIA

Task 2 (20 marks)

(a)

The Administrator is an insolvency practitioner appointed by the company to deal with the affairs of the insolvent company. The principle role of the Administrative Receiver is to secure the best outcome for his appointer albeit retaining a limited duty of care to the remaining creditors of the company. ☐

Administrative Receivership is the appointment of an insolvency practitioner by a creditor who holds a fixed charge over the assets of the company. The principal role of the Administrative Receiver is to secure the best outcome for his appointer albeit retaining a limited duty of care to the remaining creditors of the company. ☐

Administrative Receiver is the appointment of an insolvency practitioner by a creditor who holds a floating charge over the assets of the company. The principal role of the Administrative Receiver is to secure the best outcome for his appointer albeit retaining a limited duty of care to remaining creditors of the company. ☑

Administrative Receivership is a process requiring a licensed insolvency practitioner to act as the Administrator appointed by the court. The court appointed Administrator takes over the management of the company and takes responsibility for the restructuring the company or business. ☐

(b)

An action for specific performance ☐

An administration order ☐

A winding up order ☐

An action for price ☑

(c)

A court order requesting that a company make payment directly to the creditor. ☐

A court order authorising bailiffs to enter business premises and seize goods which will then be sold to settle a debt. ☑

A court order authorising liquidators to recover property under a retention of title clause and return the property to the creditor. ☐

A court order authorising creditors to enter business premises and seize goods which will then be sold to settle a debt. ☐

(d) **Retention of title will normally be valid if:**

The contract contains a retention of title clause and the goods have been delivered. ☐

The goods cannot be identified and have been converted. ☐

The retention of title clause has been included in the contract and the goods are identifiable. ☑

The goods have been bolted onto a larger piece of equipment and therefore are now part of the new equipment. ☐

(e) **In order to petition the court for a winding up order, the creditor must be owed:**

At least £750 ☑

At least £7,500 ☐

At least £750 but less than £75,000 ☐

Between £75 and £750 ☐

(f) **The receivable collection period in days for the amount owing by Jonny is**
50 **days.**

(g)

Aged trade receivables analysis ☐

Management accounts ☑

Trading history ☐

Copies of purchase orders ☑

(h) **The simple annual interest rate of the discount is** 19.60 **%.**

(i) **Complete the following sentence.**

The maximum amount available to borrow at the 30 June 20X3 is 900,000 and the product is a factoring facility ▼

BPP LEARNING MEDIA

Task 3 (24 marks)

(a)

X Limited	20X2	20X2	20X1	20X1
	Indicator	Rating	Indicator	Rating
Operating profit margin %	-6	-5	-5	-5
Interest cover	0	-30	0	-30
Current ratio	2	10	1.50	10
Gearing %	95.53	-100	90	-100
Total credit rating		-125		-125

(b)

Customer	Decision
X Limited	Reject ▼

Task 4 (24 marks)

(a)

Z Limited	20X2	20X1
	Indicator	Indicator
Gross profit margin %	25.40	23.45
Operating profit margin %	0	0
Trade payables payment period in days	121.34	89.73
Inventory holding period in days	74.97	70.23
Current ration	1.35	2
Quick ratio	0.73	1.22

(b)

Email

To:	Credit controller	**Date:**	Today
From:	AAT Technician	**Subject:**	New Customer Z Limited

Please find below my observations and recommendation for new customer Z Limited.

Profitability

The revenue has decreased by | 9.82 | % which means that the company has
either sold fewer units or decreased the price of its product. ▼

The gross profit margin has increased | 8.31 | %. The company has
Increased the sales price of the product. ▼

The company is loss making at the operational level with the operating loss £40,000 in 20X2.

This may be a problem depending on the cash flow of the business. ▼

Liquidity

The current ratio provides | a rough measure of the short term solvency of the organisation ▼

In this case it has fallen and is | still greater than 1 which is a good sign. ▼

The inventory level has | decreased. ▼

This is a good sign but the holding period has increased which means inventory may be slow moving. ▼

The quick ratio has fallen below 1 which is a major concern and supports the conclusion of poor liquidity. ▼

The trade payables payment period in days has | increased ▼ by | 31.61 | days.

It appears that the company may have insufficient liquidity and is unlikely to pay its liabilities as they fall due. ▼

I recommend that | credit not be given ▼

BPP
LEARNING MEDIA

Task 5 (24 marks)

The company turnover has increased by 44% from £6.5 million to £11.7 million. This is a strong sign of overtrading.

- You are correct that the turnover has increased but your calculation of the percentage is not correct.

- The actual percentage increase is 80%.

- The fact that the turnover has increased significantly is not a strong sign of overtrading as many indicators have to be considered to demonstrate overtrading.

- These include significant increases in turnover linked to reduced margins, increased levels of current assets and trade cycle days and cash flow lightening.

- These will be considered in turn below.

The operating profit has increased by £470,000 to £1,450,000. This means that more cash is available to pay debts.

- You are correct that the operating profit has increased by nearly £1 million.

- However, this does not mean more cash is available to pay debts. It all depends on where the profit has gone in the period.

- Has it been "invested" or "tied up" in inventory, trade receivables or non-current assets?

- This is why it is necessary to consider the liquidity of the business and changes in the assets and liabilities to confirm the liquidity of the business.

- All that can be said is that the operating profit margin has increased which gives comfort that the business has not chased turnover at the expense of profits.

- Although the gross profit margin is down slightly indicating some marginal discounting to aid demand and/or small changes to the variable costs/fixed production costs.

- Discounts do not appear to have been given, or if they have the volume increase had resulted in economies of scale with regard to production costs and non-production costs.

The interest cover has increased from 2.35 times to 4.83 times which means that the company is in a worse position than last year.

- This is not correct.

- The interest cover is a calculation of how many times the operating profit can cover the interest payments.

- It is a key indicator that credit assessment agencies and financial institutions use.

- The calculation of 4.83 times indicators that the interest paid is covered by operating profit by nearly 5x. Or, that the interest paid is just over 20% of the operating profits.

- This is an improvement and is therefore a positive sign.

- However, care needs to be taken because as we may see later operating profit does not necessarily equate to the change in cash in the period.

- And cash generation is needed to pay interest. Many profitable companies go bust because they cannot generate cash.

The current ratio should be 2 which means that last year the company was insolvent but this year the company is solvent.

- You refer to the fact that the current ratio should be 2. This is a common misunderstanding caused by several basic accounting textbooks stating that the best current ratio is at least 2.

- It is a nonsense to suggest that there is a perfect current ratio. All that can be said is that everything else being equal, the higher the ratio the better, from a credit assessment perspective.

- The current ratio is a crude measure of solvency and in this case a ratio of 4 times is a significant improvement on the previous year of 1.

- But the components of the current assets need to be considered to determine liquidity.

- The cash balance of £600,000 is a significant change from an overdraft of £1.2 million which is a very strong indicator of improved liquidity.

The trade receivables have increased by £1,200,000 which supports the conclusion of overtrading.

- The fact that the trade receivables have increased does demonstrate an application of funds (perhaps the profit increase seen earlier)

- However, the receivable days needs to be considered to support overtrading or provide comfort that the company is managing its increased levels of trade.

- In this case the trade receivable days have increased from 67 to 75 (12%).

- This indicator does show that the receivables are taking a little longer to pay than the previous year and could be an early warning sign of problems with credit control.

The trade payables are down from 68 days to 50 days implying that the company is struggling to get credit from its suppliers.

- This may not be a fair way to interpret this indicator.

- It may be that the business cash flow has improved (as indicated by the change in cash from an overdraft of £1.2 million to a cash balance of £600,000).

The inventory has increased by £600,000 which supports the conclusion of overtrading.

- It is not correct to simply say inventory has increased by a significant amount which supports overtrading.

- Because as turnover grows rapidly inventory levels would normally increase.

- However, it is correct to say that the working capital requirement has needed another £600,000 of funding.

- The important indicator is inventory holding period which has actually reduced slightly to 63 days which is a positive sign.

Gearing has decreased which means that the banks are not happy to lend money to the business.

- You are correct that the gearing level has decreased from 83.33% to 73.39%.

- This does not necessarily mean that the banks are unhappy to lend to the business

- It may be that the business does not need to increase the level of borrowing

- What is of more importance is the fact that the profile of the debt has improved by converting short term overdraft to a long term loan.

- This has aided liquidity

- But may be deferring cash flow problems to future years.

- Interestingly the long term loans are greater than the non-current assets, so the increase in long term debt is financing the increase in current assets. This may be a concern.

- **My conclusion is that credit should be given.**

- **On balance there are several warning signs (significant increase in turnover linked with funds being absorbed into inventory and receivables, with borrowing at significant levels)**

- **And several positive signs (growing turnover linked to increasing profitability, liquidity improving with cash in the bank, payable days reducing)**

- **It is probably worth visiting the customer to understand the medium term forecast and the cash position in the coming 12 months.**

- **Also we need to understand the strategy with regard to borrowing**

....

Task 6 (18 marks)

Customer A

The balance on Customer A's account is £24,500 This consists of two invoices, one for £17,250 which is not overdue and one for £7,250 which is overdue. An unallocated payment has been received for £7,250 and posted to the unallocated payment accounts in the purchase ledger. It has now been identified as a receipt from Customer A.

The action needed is to

credit customer A's account with £7,250 and debit un allocated payments with £7,250.	▼

Customer B

This is a new customer who placed their first order a few weeks ago. The goods were delivered on 1 September 20X3 and the invoice was raised on 10 September 20X3 on 30 day terms.

The account should be put on stop. ☐

The account is not overdue so no action is required. ☑

The customer should be contacted and an immediate payment requested. ☐

A phone call should have been made on 17 September 20X3 and a letter sent on 24 September 20X3. ☐

Customer C

A balance of £36,250 is 64 days overdue and is for one invoice. Customer C claims that the goods were not received.

Send the original delivery note signed by Customer C. ☐

Raise a credit note for £36,250. ☐

Send a copy of the signed delivery note which was signed by Customer C. ☑

Send a copy of the signed delivery note signed by the courier who delivered the package. ☐

Customer D

Customer D sent a payment of £25,000 but did not provide details of which invoices the payment relates to.

Customer D should be contacted to confirm which invoices are being paid so that the unallocated receipt can be allocated. ☑

The £25,000 should be returned to Customer D. ☐

The £25,000 should be allocated to the last invoices first. ☐

The £25,000 should be posted to unallocated payments. ☐

BPP
LEARNING MEDIA

Customer E

Customer E owes a balance of £55,200 including VAT. The account is on stop. Attempts to contact the customer by telephone and letter have been unsuccessful. The account is credit insured.

Complete the sentence below.

Contact the credit insurer to make a claim that for: £ [36800] , make a provision for: £ [9200] and claim VAT of: £ [9200] from HMRC.

Customer F

Customer F has gone into administration after being a customer for five years. Up until six months ago, they had always paid to terms.

Place the account on stop and contact a debt collection company to deal with processing a claim against Customer F. ☐

Contact the insolvency service and register a claim with the credit insurer. ☐

Visit premises of Customer F and seize goods to the value of the outstanding balance. ☐

Contact the insolvency practitioner and register a claim with the credit insurer. ☑

....

Task 7 (18 marks)

(a) **Botton Ltd**

- The account should be on stop because the debt is more than 28 days overdue.

- The company may be using the online banking problem as a delaying tactic.

- Moss Ltd should contact Botton Ltd and ask them to make payment by cheque or to go into the bank and make a CHAPS transfer.

- Alternatively a member of staff from Moss Ltd could visit the premises of Botton Ltd to collect a cheque or collect cash.

- If these options are not acceptable to Botton Ltd then it may be necessary to provide for an irrecoverable debt of £12,000 and make a credit insurance claim of £28,000.

- VAT of £8,000 may be reclaimed from HMRC once the debt is six months overdue and has been written off in the company's accounts.

- The debt should be placed in the hands of a debt collection agency if payment is not forthcoming.

Hamiltons

- All products manufactured by Moss Ltd have a batch number stamped on them and so they should be easily identifiable.

- Moss should be assertive with the receiver and insist that they be allowed to visit the premises to attempt to identify goods supplied by Moss.

- Receivers often attempt to avoid ROT claims be initially stating that the claim is not valid in the hope that the supplier will not pursue the claim any further.

- The threat of legal action can be used if the receiver is not cooperating with a possible identification visit.

- The credit insurance company often have a specialist insolvency section who themselves are often ex insolvency practitioners / specialists.

- Moss Ltd or the credit insurer should therefore visit Hamiltons premises immediately to identify any goods still on the premises so that an ROT claim can be made.

- The receiver should be present to confirm identification if possible

- The credit insurer should be contacted and a claim made for £10,500,
    - A provision for an irrecoverable debt of £4,500 should be made
    - And VAT of £3,000 will be reclaimable from HMRC.

Schumaker & Co

- Moss Ltd should review the order from Schumaker to determine which product was ordered.

- If the order was for BP20 then Schumaker will need to pay for the goods to be returned and pay the restocking fee of 10% if they do not want the goods.

- If they wish to keep the goods then Moss Ltd can enforce the contract for payment.

- If Moss Ltd believes that the debt will not be paid even if the error was down to Schumaker then it may be more beneficial for Moss Ltd to collect the goods and resell them rather than try and collect the debt.

- If the error was made by Moss Ltd then the goods should be collected and a credit note should be raised.

- In addition if the error is due to Moss Ltd then they should waive the restocking fee.

- The fact that Schumaker is an important customer may mean that Moss Ltd may decide to take a lenient approach if it was Schumaker who is at fault.

- Moss may decide that as a goodwill gesture the restocking fee will be waived, and also perhaps the collection fee.

- It may be that the customer profitability in the course of the year is many times the additional cost if Moss waives the charges.

(b)   £150,000 plus £50,000 × 1.2 (£60,000) less £150,000 − £48,000 + £4,800 = £16,800 at 31 March 20X3

£16,800 plus £80,400 less £24,000 less £90,000 = £16,800 in credit at 30 April 20X3

(c)   •   Invoice date 15 March − The order should not have been accepted because the credit limit is £20,000 and this order has exceeded it.

•   Invoice dated 15 March − £26,000 plus VAT = £31,200 amount due for payment by 14 April.

•   Telephone call should have been made on 21 April.

•   Letter should have been sent on 28 April.

•   Account should have been placed on stop on 12 May.

•   Order delivered on 4 May should not have been accepted because the credit limit of £20,000 has been exceeded.

•   Invoice from 5 May was due for payment 4 June.

•   Telephone call should have been made on 11 June.

•   Letter should have been sent on 18 June.

BPP
LEARNING MEDIA

BPP PRACTICE ASSESSMENT 1
CREDIT CONTROL

Time allowed: 2 hours 30 minutes

BPP PRACTICE ASSESSMENT 1
CREDIT CONTROL

Time allowed: 2 hours 30 minutes

Task 1a

A cosmetics business produces and distributes a monthly catalogue to all the households in its local area to introduce its new products. The catalogue includes a price list and an order form. After a week the catalogues are collected along with any orders that have been placed.

In terms of contract law, how would you describe the business' distribution of the catalogue?

An intention to create legal relations ☐

An invitation to treat ☐

An offer ☐

A tender ☐

Task 1b

Jane goes into the florist to buy some flowers that are advertised in the window as being on special offer at £5 a bunch. Inside the shop she finds that the advertised flowers are sold out and the cheapest bunches available are £7.50. Jane demands that the florist sell her the more expensive flowers at £5 but the florist refuses.

Which of the following statements is correct?

The advert is an invitation to treat and the florist's failure to make the advertised flowers available renders it a defective contract. ☐

The advert is an offer and the florist's failure to make the advertised flowers available is a breach of contract. ☐

The advert is an offer and Jane's demand that the florist sell her the more expensive flowers at £5 is a revocation of an offer. ☐

The advert is an invitation to treat and Jane's demand to buy the more expensive flowers at £5 is an offer which is rejected by the florist. ☐

Task 1c

Which of the following best describes consideration?

The payment of cash ☐

The promise of an exchange of value ☐

The intention for the parties to be legally bound ☐

The absolute and unqualified acceptance of both parties ☐

Task 1d

Which of the following statements concerning contractual terms are incorrect?

(i)   Terms are usually classified as either conditions or warranties.

(ii) If a condition in a contract is not fulfilled the whole contract is said to be discharged by breach.

(iii) If a warranty in a contract is not fulfilled the whole contract is said to be discharged by breach.

(i) only ☐

(ii) only ☐

(i) and (iii) only ☐

(iii) only ☐

Task 1e

Which of the following is not an essential element for a contract to be formed and valid?

The promise of an exchange of value ☐

The contract must be in writing ☐

The intention for the parties to be legally bound ☐

A valid offer and acceptance ☐

Task 1f

A business accepts a telephone order from John, to deliver a box of computer games the next day for £60. Before delivery however the business is informed by another customer that John is still a minor.

In terms of contract law, how would you describe this contract?

An illegal contract ☐

A void contract ☐

A voidable contract ☐

An unenforceable contract ☐

Task 1g

Jude goes into a shop and sees a price label for £200 on a dishwasher. She agrees to buy the dishwasher but the till operator tells her that the label is misprinted and should read £300. Jude maintains that she only has to pay £200.

How would you describe the price on the price label in terms of contract law?

An acceptance ☐

An invitation to treat ☐

An offer ☐

A tender ☐

Task 1h

Which of the following is not a remedy for breach of contract?

Quantum meruit ☐

Specific performance ☐

Petition for an administration order ☐

Injunction ☐

Task 1i

Which of the following is not one of the three key prerequisites for goods under the Sale of Goods Act?

Satisfactory quality ☐

Fit for purpose ☐

Fair price ☐

As described ☐

Task 1j

Which of the following legislation only gives rights to individuals, not companies?

Trade Descriptions Act ☐

Unfair Contract Terms Act ☐

Late Payment of Commercial Debts (Interest) Act ☐

Consumer Credit Act ☐

Task 1k

Consider the following statements made in connection with the Data Protection Act:

(i)   "Personal information" includes expressions of opinion as well as factual information held about a living individual.

(ii) A "data subject" is a person who holds and processes personal information.

Which statements are true?

(i) only ☐

(ii) only ☐

Both statements ☐

Neither statement ☐

Task 1l

The following is a description of one of the seven rights of data subjects under the Data Protection Act.

"Anyone can ask a data controller not to process data relating to them that causes substantial unwarranted distress to them or anyone else."

Which right is being described?

Right to prevent processing ☐

Right to subject access ☐

Right to rectification, blocking, erasure and destruction ☐

Right to compensation ☐

Task 2a

Alpha Limited has supplied goods on credit to a self-employed plumber, but the debt of £800 remains unpaid, despite issuing a statutory demand for payment.

In terms of the next step, what can Alpha Ltd approach the Court for?

A petition for bankruptcy ☐

Appointment of a liquidator ☐

An attachment of earnings order ☐

Appointment of an insolvency practitioner ☐

Task 2b

What does the Late Payment of Commercial Debts Act allow?

A supplier must offer a purchaser a settlement discount. ☐

A supplier can insist upon a settlement discount being taken by the purchaser. ☐

A purchaser can only pay for goods after the credit term if agreed with the supplier. ☐

A supplier can charge interest on overdue amounts owing. ☐

Task 2c

Conrad Ltd is refusing to pay an outstanding invoice of £5,500 to Wiggins plc.

Which of the following courts would deal with any legal action brought by Wiggins plc to enforce payment of the debt?

County Court ☐

High Court ☐

Small Claims court ☐

Industrial tribunal ☐

Task 2d

The purpose of a first reminder letter to an overdue receivable is:

To threaten legal action ☐

To notify the customer that a debt collection agency has been appointed ☐

To inform the customer that no further sales will be made to them ☐

To clarify the amount due and when it was due and to encourage payment ☐

Task 2e

Which of the following is not a recognised type of credit insurance?

Third party policy ☐

Whole turnover policy ☐

Annual aggregate excess policy ☐

Specific receivables ☐

Task 2f

A company's stated credit terms are Net 30 days, 2% discount for payment after 10 days. One of its customers, Company Z, which always takes the discount offered, has received an invoice for £200.

What is the simple annual interest rate for the settlement discount?

37.2% ☐

36.5% ☐

24.8% ☐

24.3% ☐

Task 2g

What is the main purpose of offering a settlement discount to customers?

To increase sales ☐

To increase the number of customers ☐

To save on interest costs ☐

To earn higher profit ☐

Task 2h

Which of the following services is unlikely to be available from a debt factoring company?

Administration of the receivables' ledger ☐

An advance of finance in respect of a certain percentage of receivables ☐

Insurance against irrecoverable debts ☐

Seizure of property from customers who refuse to pay ☐

Task 2i

Which of the following is an advantage of debt factoring but not an advantage of invoice discounting?

Cash advance provided ☐

Useful for fast growing company ☐

Administration of sales ledger by an expert in debt collection ☐

Confidential agreement so will not affect customer goodwill ☐

Task 2j

A customer's outstanding balance at 31 December 20X1 has been analysed as follows:

19/09/X1	Invoice 175	610
23/09/X1	Invoice 177	667
23/09/X1	Credit note for goods returned	-31
10/10/X1	Invoice 178	894
21/11/X1	Invoice 179	561
Balance outstanding		**2,701**

What is the amount that would appear in the aged receivables' analysis as more than 90 days outstanding?

£1,246 ☐

£1,308 ☐

£2,140 ☐

£2,202 ☐

Task 3a

Which of the following sources of information constitute external sources for assessing a customer's credit status?

(i)   Bank reference
(ii) Visit to customer
(iii) Sales representative's knowledge
(iv) Credit agency reference
(v)   Trade reference
(vi) Analysis of recent financial statements

(i), (ii), (iv) and (v)   ☐

(i), (ii), (iv), and (vi)   ☐

(i), (iv) and (v)   ☐

(i), (iii), (iv),(v) and (vi)   ☐

Task 3b

A customer places an order for £3,000 which means that the balance on the customer's receivables ledger will be £10,000 whereas the credit limit for this customer is £12,000.

What action would be required?

Despatch the goods to the customer   ☐

Put a stop on the customer's account   ☐

Discuss the situation with the customer   ☐

Make an allowance for a doubtful debt   ☐

Task 3c

Which of the following is the correct description of a credit circle?

A commercial organisation which provides credit status information about companies and individuals.   ☐

The time taken between a business paying for its raw materials and receiving cash in from the customer for the sale of the product.   ☐

A group of companies, often operating in the same industry, who share information on current and prospective customers for credit purposes.   ☐

The steps that a business goes through between the customer receiving an invoice for a credit sale and the cash being received by the business.   ☐

Task 3d

The following bank references have been received in relation to four customers:

Customer W	Considered good for your purposes
Customer X	Well constituted business with capital seemingly fully employed
Customer Y	Should prove good for your figures
Customer Z	Unable to speak for your figures

Which is the correct ranking of the customers in terms of the risk of granting credit, starting with the least risky?

W,X,Y,Z ☐

W,Y,X,Z ☐

Y,W,X,Z ☐

Y,X,W Z ☐

Task 3e

The 80/20 rule for analysing receivables is:

An approach intended to ensure that 80% of the time only 20% of the receivables are more than 60 days old. ☐

An approach that suggests 20 out of every 100 customers will default at some point. ☐

An approach that suggests on average 20% of customers make up 80% of the total receivables. ☐

An approach that suggests a business splits its aged receivables analysis between accounts that are less than 20 days old, 20-80 days old and more than 80 days overdue. ☐

Task 4a

You work as a credit control manager for Cameron Ltd, which has the following credit control policy for assessing customer credit applications:

Cameron Ltd credit control policy for assessing customer credit applications

New accounts

1   One bank reference and two trade references are required for all customers.

2   A credit reference agency report and the last two years' published financial statements for limited companies needs to be analysed.

3   A credit reference agency report and the last three years' financial statements for a sole trader need to be analysed.

Existing customers

4   A credit reference agency report to be obtained on an annual basis together with the latest annual financial statements (either from Companies House or directly from the customer). Both documents to be reviewed.

5   A trading history review to be undertaken annually to review the performance against credit limits and terms of payment

6   Annual review of usage of the customers' credit limit and to ensure that an outdated credit limit is not in existence. This is particularly important where the trade with the customer has reduced over the past.

All customers

7   Cameron Ltd will assess the risk of default for both new and existing customers by monitoring certain key ratios: operating profit margin, current ratio, payables' turnover, gearing and interest cover.

8   After consideration of the evidence above, each application is to be designated Low, Medium or High risk.

Assume it is 31 March 20X8.

You have received applications for credit from John Roberts, a sole trader, who operates as a painter and decorator. John is a prospective new customer and is seeking a credit limit of £1,000 and 30 day payment terms. Supporting information for the application is as follows.

Information to support John Roberts Application

John Roberts: Financial statements year ending 30 September 20X7

Statement of profit or loss year ending 30 September 20X7

	£
Revenue	95,000
Cost of sales	(32,000)
Gross profit	63,000
Operating expenses	(35,500)
Profit	27,500

Statement of Financial Position at 30 September 20X7

	£	£
Non-current assets		12,500
Current assets		
Inventory	2,300	
Receivables	6,000	
Cash	500	
		8,800
Current liabilities		(2,750)
Net current assets		6,050
Total assets less current liabilities		18,550
Capital and reserves		18,550

Big Bank

Monnow Way

Bristol

BS7 6TY

Credit Control Manager

Cameron Ltd

Tregarn Trading Estate

Cardiff

CF1 3EW
                                                                  22 March 20X8

Dear Sir/Madam

In response to your request for credit information on John Roberts we can confirm that the customer's credit of £1,000 is considered good for your purposes.

Yours faithfully

A Evans

Bank Manager

We have received a request for credit from John Roberts who has quoted yourselves as a referee. We would be grateful if you could answer the following questions and return in the stamped addressed envelope enclosed.

Your Business	P Conneely & Sons
How long has the customer been trading with you?	Two years
Your credit terms with customer per month	£2,000
Period of credit granted	45 days
Payment record	Prompt/occasionally late/slow
Have you ever suspended credit to the customer?	Yes/No
Any other relevant information	No

We have received a request for credit from John Roberts who has quoted yourselves as a referee. We would be grateful if you could answer the following questions and return in the stamped addressed envelope enclosed.

Your Business	JW Thompson Ltd
How long has the customer been trading with you?	Four years
Your credit terms with customer per month	£1,000
Period of credit granted	30 days
Payment record	Prompt/occasionally late/slow
Have you ever suspended credit to the customer?	Yes/No
If yes – when and for how long?	In the first year of trading for 3 months, but nothing in the last three years
Any other relevant information	John is a regular customer – he experienced some cash flow difficulties when he first started trading but in the last 3 years has proved to be one of our best paying customers

Using the financial statements provided, complete the tables of key ratios set out below.

Key ratios: John Roberts	Year ended 30 September		
	20X7	20X6	20X5
Operating profit margin (%) (to 1dp)		25.2	Information not provided by customer
Current ratio : 1 (to 1dp)		2.8	
Accounts payable payment period (nearest day)		29	

BPP LEARNING MEDIA

Task 4b

Using your answer to Task 4a and all the other available information, carry out a full assessment of John Robert's application for credit, in accordance with Cameron Ltd's credit control policy, recording your results as appropriate. Recommend, with reasons, whether the requested credit limit should be granted and specify any further action that needs to be taken.

Complete the following summary of your decisions for the financial controller.

Risk assessment	Risk level	Decision re credit
John Roberts	▼	▼

Picklist – Risk level
High
Medium
Low

Picklist – Decision
Accept
Reject

Task 5a

Jemima Ltd is a potential new commercial customer which has previously bought goods from one of your competitors. Jemima Ltd wishes to open an account with your company with a credit limit of £10,000 and wants you to match your competitor's 60 day payment terms. The sales department are very keen to do business with Jemima Ltd and are exerting pressure on you to process the application quickly.

The following information relates to the application.

Jemima Ltd: Summarised Financial Statements year ended 30 November 20X7

Statement of profit or loss

Year ended 30 November 20X7

	£'000
Sales revenue	2,360
Cost of sales	1,690
Gross profit	**670**
Operating expenses	580
Profit from operations	**90**
Finance costs (interest payable)	40
Profit from operations before tax	**50**
Tax	12
Profit for the period	**38**

Jemima Ltd: Summarised Statement of financial position at

30 November 20X7
£'000

ASSETS	
Non-current assets	741
Current assets:	
Inventory	280
Receivables	450
Cash at bank	2
	732
Total assets	**1,473**
EQUITY AND LIABILITIES	
Equity	
Ordinary share capital	100
Retained earnings	315
Total equity	**415**
Non-current liabilities	
Long-term loans	600
Current liabilities	
Trade payables	370
Other payables	88
	458
Total liabilities	**1,058**
Total equity and liabilities	**1,473**

Timely Bank

Clifton Way

Bristol

BS7 1EW

Credit Control Manager

Cameron Ltd

Tregarn Trading Estate

Cardiff

CF1 3EW

28 March 20X8

Dear Sir/Madam

In response to your request for credit information on Jemima Ltd we can confirm that this is a well constituted business with capital seeming to be fully employed. We do not think that the directors would undertake a commitment they could not fulfil.

Yours faithfully

L Nelson

Bank Manager

We have received a request for credit from Jemima Ltd who has quoted yourselves as a referee. We would be grateful if you could answer the following questions and return in the stamped addressed envelope enclosed.

Your Business	Dreammakers Ltd
How long has the customer been trading with you?	Two years
Your credit terms with customer per month	£12,000
Period of credit granted	45 days
Payment record	Prompt/occasionally late/slow
Have you ever suspended credit to the customer?	Yes/No
If yes – when and for how long?	Last year for six months
Any other relevant information	

We have received a request for credit from Jemima Ltd who has quoted yourselves as a referee. We would be grateful if you could answer the following questions and return in the stamped addressed envelope enclosed.

Your Business	Fox and Co
How long has the customer been trading with you?	Four years
Your credit terms with customer per month	£15,000
Period of credit granted	<u>60 days</u>
Payment record	<u>Prompt</u>/ occasionally late /slow
Have you ever suspended credit to the customer?	Yes/<u>No</u>
If yes – when and for how long?	
Any other relevant information	

Using the financial statements provided, complete the tables of key ratios set out below.

Key ratios: Jemima Ltd	Year ended 30 November		
	20X7	20X6	20X5
Operating profit margin (%) (to 1dp)		4.2	Information not provided by customer
Current ratio : 1 (to 2dp)		1.75	
Accounts payable payment period (nearest day)		65	
Gearing (total debt/(total debt + equity)) % (to 1dp)		48.0	
Interest cover (times to 2dp)		2.9 times	

BPP
LEARNING MEDIA

Task 5b

Using your answer to 5a and the information provided in 5a, complete the notes below providing an assessment of Jemima Ltd and concluding with a decision in respect of Jemima Ltd's request for credit.

Notes

Commentary on ratios

Looking at the accounting ratios they indicate (1) [▼]

The company is profitable but the operating profit margin has (2) [▼] .

The current ratio is low and the payables payment period is (3) [▼] and is

(4) [▼] the credit terms requested.

The gearing ratio is (5) [▼] , whilst interest cover, which is still acceptable,

is decreasing. The fact interest cover is decreasing (6) [▼] .

The financial analysis is indicative of a business that (7) [▼] .

Picklists – commentary on ratios

(1)   A decline in performance between 20X6 and 20X7 / an improvement in performance between 20X6 and 20X7 / no change in performance between 20X6 and 20X7.

(2)   Increased /decreased / remained unchanged

(3)   Increasing / decreasing /unchanged

(4)   Higher / lower

(5)   Relatively low but increasing / relatively high and increasing / relatively high but decreasing

(6)   Is a good sign / is not a good sign

(7)   Is unlikely to have cash flow problems / may be having cash flow problems

Notes continued

References

The bank reference is (1) [▼]. The bank's comments suggests that they

(2) [▼].

Both trade referees have granted Jemima Ltd more credit than Jemima is currently seeking from us. The trade reference from Fox and Co (who trade on 60 days, limit £15,000) is

(3) [▼] whilst that from Dreammakers is the opposite.

This (4) [▼] on the reliability of the references.

Picklists – References

(1)   Favourable / not favourable

(2)   Have no concerns about the business' cash flow / have concerns about the business' cash flow

(3)   Positive / worrying

(4)   Enhances / casts doubt on

Notes continued

Summary

The customer is deemed to be (1) [▼] based on financial analysis and references therefore credit should be (2) [▼].

Picklists – Summary

(1)   High risk / low risk

(2)   Granted / refused

BPP
LEARNING MEDIA

Task 6

August Ltd, an existing customer, wishes to extend their credit limit from £20,000 to £25,000, under their existing 45 day terms. Ratio analysis of their last three years of financial statements has already been carried out as below.

August Ltd	20X7	20X6	20X5
Operating profit margin	6.4%	6%	5.6%
Current ratio	2.1	1.97	1.9
Accounts payable payment period	33 days	38 days	32 days
Gearing (total debt/(total debt + equity))	25%	25%	0%
Interest cover	4 times	3.5 times	n/a

Information relevant to August Ltd's Application

Analysis of August Ltd's receivables ledger January- December 20X7

August Ltd	Total receivables balance as at last working day of month	Analysed as:		Maximum balance outstanding at any point in the month
		0-30 days	30-60 days	
	£	£	£	£
January	18,500	16,000	2,500	18,973
February	9,204	7,000	2,204	11,204
March	12,200	12,200		14,678
April	17,426	10,000	7,426	19,234
May	18,345	13,345	5,000	18,345
June	14,365	14,365		19,870
July	15,000	15,000		18,766
August	13,600	10,200	3,400	14,567
September	16,400	8,400	8,000	18,345
October	16,800	9,800	7,000	17,398
November	18,500	18,500		19,779
December	17,120	11,500	5,620	19,234

In respect of August Ltd recommend, with reasons, whether the requested credit limits should be granted and specify any further action that needs to be taken.

Task 7a

An extract of Cameron Ltd's credit control policy is set out below:

Debt collection process

1   Invoices to be raised and sent to customer within one day of goods being delivered

2   Statements to be despatched on last working day of the month

3   Aged receivables' analysis to be produced monthly. Computer will automatically generate an exception report of all accounts that do not comply with credit terms, which must be reviewed and actioned.

4   Reminder letter to be sent immediately an account is overdue

5   Telephone reminder for accounts 10 days overdue

6   Customer on stop list if no payment is received within five days of the telephone reminder. Computerised sales order processing system updated and automatic e-mail sent to the customer and to the account manager within our sales department

7   Letter threatening legal action if payment not received within 30 days of the first letter

8   Legal proceedings/debt collection agency instructed subject to approval of the finance director once debt is more than 45 days overdue

9   If at any stage in the process the customer is declared insolvent or bankrupt then contact the insolvency practitioner in order to register the debt and notify the financial accountant so that the sales tax can be reclaimed.

Your assistant is responsible for reviewing the aged receivables' analysis. You have received the following exception report from them, together with their notes and any suggestions for follow-up. However you know from past experience their suggested actions are not always the most appropriate actions in the circumstances.

EXCEPTION REPORT BASED ON AGED RECEIVABLES' ANALYSIS as at 31 March 20X8

The following customers are in breach of their credit terms:

Customer	Note	Credit terms	Credit limit £	Amount due £	Current £	31–60 days £	61–90 days £
Brianne Ltd	1	30 days	2,000.00	2,500.00	2,500		
Roxy plc	2	45 days	15,000.00	13,250.00	11,000		2,250
Statham and Sons	3	30 days	20,000.00	16,820.00		16,820	
Flames Ltd	4	60 days	25,000.00	16,815.75	6,815.75	7,500	2,500
Ice Ltd	5	60 days	25,000.00	8,000.00	(15,000)	13,000	10,000

Notes and Suggested actions

(1) Brianne Ltd – No action required as the amount outstanding is all current.

(2) Roxy plc – They dispute the invoice for £2,250, claiming never to have received the goods concerned. We cannot trace our copy of the signed delivery note. They are a regular customer, we normally have no problems dealing with them and the rest of the account is up to date.

(3) Statham and Sons – This is one invoice dated 10 February 20X8. I phoned them over a week ago and they said the cheque is in the post.

(4) Flames Ltd – The invoice for £2,500 is dated 28 January 20X8. I heard from a friend of mine that one of Flames Ltd's major customers has recently gone into liquidation and that Flames Ltd are experiencing cash flow difficulties as a result.

(5) Ice Ltd – We recently received a payment of £15,000 but it does not specify which invoices it relates to. Suggest we allocate against the oldest debts first and then this account will be OK.

Review the exception report prepared by your assistant and complete the table below by selecting the appropriate action from the picklist for each customer account.

Customer	Action	
Brianne Ltd		▼
Roxy plc		▼
Statham and Sons		▼
Flames Ltd		▼
Ice Ltd		▼

BPP LEARNING MEDIA

Picklists:

Brianne Ltd

The account is not overdue so no action is required

This customer should be put on the stop list which will result in them receiving an automatic e mail.

The account balance is not overdue but the account should be investigated since the credit limit has been exceeded.

Roxy plc

An allowance should be made for £2,250.

This customer should be put on the stop list which will result in them receiving an automatic e mail.

No action is necessary as we normally have no problems dealing with them

Statham and Sons

No action is necessary.

This customer should be put on the stop list which will result in them receiving an automatic e mail.

Wait another week to see if the cheque arrives before deciding on further action.

Flames Ltd

No action is necessary.

Inform Flames you can no longer trade with them as they are considered too risky.

Contact Flames to discuss the situation, then reconsider their credit status with us.

Ice Ltd

Allocate the £15,000 against the oldest debts first

Contact the customer and ask them to confirm which invoices the £15,000 relates to before deciding on appropriate action.

Allocate the £15,000 against the newest debts first to be prudent

Task 7b

A credit control policy and an extract from an aged receivables' analysis are set out below.

CREDIT CONTROL POLICY

1. Invoices must be issued on the same day as goods are despatched.

2. An aged analysis of trade receivables is to be produced monthly.

3. Credit terms are strictly 30 days from the date of invoice.

4. Statements are despatched on the first working day of each month.

5. A reminder letter must be sent when a debt is 14 days overdue.

6. A telephone call to chase payment must be made when a debt is 21 days overdue.

7. The customer will be placed on the stop list when the debt is 30 days overdue and a meeting arranged with the customer to discuss the operation of the account.

8. A letter threatening legal action will be sent when the debt is 45 days overdue.

9. Legal proceedings are to be commenced when a debt is 60 days overdue subject to the agreement of the financial controller.

AGED RECEIVABLES' ANALYSIS – EXTRACT AT 30 JUNE 20X6

	Total	Credit limit	Current <30 days	31–60 days	61–90 days	90 days
	£	£	£	£	£	£
Castle Builders	10,800	12,000				10,800
DD DIY Ltd	6,800	10,000	5,200	1,200		400
AP Partners	3,250	4,000	1,000	1,000	1,250	
Gatfield Ltd	17,640	25,000	8,200	8,600	840	
Kier Ltd	21,200	20,000	8,900	12,300		
Crane Co	3,200	4,000	3,200			

On the basis of the information above prepare an action plan for each receivable including:

*   **Any credit control action required for the account.**

*   **Any suggestions for allowances against doubtful debts.**

BPP PRACTICE ASSESSMENT 1
CREDIT CONTROL

ANSWERS

BPP
LEARNING MEDIA

Task 1a

The correct answer is: An invitation to treat

....

Task 1b

The correct answer is: The advert is an invitation to treat and Jane's demand to buy the more expensive flowers at £5 is an offer which is rejected by the florist.

....

Task 1c

The correct answer is: The promise of an exchange of value

....

Task 1d

The correct answer is: (iii) only

....

Task 1e

The correct answer is: The contract must be in writing

....

Task 1f

The correct answer is: A voidable contract

....

Task 1g

The correct answer is: An invitation to treat

Jude offers to buy and the till operator can accept or reject the offer.

....

Task 1h

The correct answer is: Petition for an administration order

Task 1i

The correct answer is: Fair price

Task 1j

The correct answer is: Consumer Credit Act

Task 1k

The correct answer is: (i) only

Task 1l

The correct answer is: Right to prevent processing

Task 2a

The correct answer is: A petition for bankruptcy

Task 2b

The correct answer is: A supplier can charge interest on overdue amounts owing.

Task 2c

The correct answer is: County Court

Task 2d

The correct answer is: To clarify the amount due and when it was due and to encourage payment

Task 2e

The correct answer is: Third party policy

Task 2f

The correct answer is: 37.2%

(2/98 × 365/20 × 100 = 37.2%)

Task 2g

The correct answer is: To save on interest costs

If the monies are received earlier from customers then this can be used to reduce a bank overdraft and therefore the interest cost.

Task 2h

The correct answer is: Seizure of property from customers who refuse to pay

Task 2i

The correct answer is: Administration of sales ledger by an expert in debt collection

Task 2j

The correct answer is: £1,246

Task 3a

The correct answer is: (i), (iv) and (v)

Task 3b

The correct answer is: Despatch the goods to the customer

Task 3c

The correct answer is: A group of companies, often operating in the same industry, who share information on current and prospective customers for credit purposes

Task 3d

The correct answer is: W,Y,X,Z

Task 3e

The correct answer is: An approach that suggests on average 20% of customers make up 80% of the total receivables

BPP
LEARNING MEDIA

Task 4a

Key ratios: John Roberts	Year ended 30 September		
	20X7	**20X6**	**20X5**
Operating profit margin (%) (to 1dp)	28.9	25.2	Information not provided by customer
Current ratio : 1 (to 1dp)	3.2	2.8	
Accounts payable payment period (nearest day)	31	29	

Workings

(a) Operating profit margin = 27,500/95,000 × 100% = 28.9%
(b) Current ratio = 8,800/2,750 = 3.2 : 1
(c) Accounts payable payment period = (2,750/32,000) × 365 = 31 days

Task 4b

John Roberts

Assessment

Looking at the accounting ratios:

John Roberts appears to be profitable - the operating margin has increased from 25.2% to 28.9% in 20X7. Liquidity ratios suggest the business can comfortably afford to pay its short term debts when due and its average payment period for suppliers is 31 days, which is comparable to the credit terms being sought.

The business has no debt in its capital structure and as a result there is no gearing risk.

References:

The bank reference is positive, "considered good for your purposes" is not quite as good as "undoubted" but suggests that the business is a reasonable risk.

Both trade references are positive and although credit was suspended in the early days of the business it has not happened again in the last three years since.

Decision re. credit application:

Sole trader, who operates as a painter and decorator, deemed to be low-medium risk based on financial analysis and references.

Agree to credit limit of £1,000 and 30 day payment terms subject to receipt of satisfactory credit reference agency report and also submission of accounts for the year ended 30 September 20X5.

As this is a new customer a review could be scheduled for six months.

Action required

Need to get credit reference agency report and financial statements for y/e 20X5 to comply with credit control policy (three years financial statements for sole trader)

Write to customer to communicate decision

Summary

Risk assessment	Risk level	Decision re credit
John Roberts	Low	Accept

Note: Medium risk would also be an acceptable answer.

Task 5a

Key ratios: Jemima Ltd	Year ended 30 November		
	20X7	20X6	20X5
Operating profit margin (%) (to 1dp)	3.8	4.2	Information not provided by customer
Current ratio : 1 (to 2dp)	1.60	1.75	
Accounts payable payment period (nearest day)	80	65	
Gearing (total debt/(total debt + equity)) % (to 1dp)	59.1	48.0	
Interest cover (times to 2dp)	2.25	2.90	

Workings

(a) Operating profit margin = 90/2,360 × 100% = 3.8%
(b) Current ratio = 732/458 = 1.6 : 1
(c) Accounts payable payment period = (370/1,690) × 365 = 80 days
(d) Gearing ratio = (600/(415 + 600)) × 100 = 59.1%
(e) Interest cover = 90/40 = 2.25 times

BPP LEARNING MEDIA

Task 5b

Looking at the accounting ratios they indicate **a decline in performance between 20X6 and 20X7**. The company is profitable but the operating profit margin has **decreased**.

The current ratio is low and the payables payment period is **increasing** and is **higher** than the credit terms requested. The gearing ratio is **relatively high and increasing**, whilst interest cover, which is still acceptable, is decreasing. The fact interest cover is decreasing **is not a good sign**. The financial analysis is indicative of a business that **may be having cash flow problems**.

References

The bank reference is **not favourable**. The bank's comments suggests that **they have concerns about the business' cash flow**.

Both trade referees have granted Jemima Ltd more credit than Jemima is currently seeking from us. The trade reference from Fox and Co (who trade on 60 days, limit £15,000) is **positive**, whilst that from Dreammakers is the opposite. This **casts doubt** on the reliability of the references.

Summary

The customer is deemed to be **high risk** based on financial analysis and references therefore credit should be **refused**.

••

Task 6

August Ltd

Assessment

The receivables ledger information suggests that the customer has been active throughout the year but has remained within their credit limit at all times and the aged receivables' analysis, which does not at any point have balances > 61 days, suggests that they have adhered to their 45 day terms. There may be some seasonality, with balances in February, March and August being lower, but generally the customer is making close to full use of their credit limit and this is probably why they have requested an extension.

Looking at the accounting ratios:

The company appears to be profitable and the operating margin has increased steadily since 20X5. Liquidity ratios have improved suggesting August can afford to pay its short term debts when due and its average payment period for suppliers is 33 days, which is significantly less than our terms of 45 days.

Until 20X5 the company appears to have used all equity finance. It now has some debt in its capital structure (25% gearing) but the interest cover of 4 times does not suggest that it has a problem servicing this.

Decision re. credit application:

Existing customer, deemed to be low risk based on financial analysis and existing track record

Agree to extension of credit from £20,000 to £25,000, under their existing 45 day terms, subject to satisfactory credit reference agency report, with a review in 6 months to ensure new terms are being agreed to.

Action required

Need to get credit reference agency report to comply with credit control policy

Write to customer to communicate decision

Task 7a

Review of assistant's exception report

Customer	Action
Brianne Ltd	The account balance is not overdue but the account should be investigated since the credit limit has been exceeded.
Roxy plc	An allowance should be made for £2,250.
Statham and Sons	This customer should be put on the stop list which will result in them receiving an automatic e mail.
Flames Ltd	Contact Flames to discuss the situation, then reconsider their credit status with us.
Ice Ltd	Contact the customer and ask them to confirm which invoices the £15,000 relates to before deciding on appropriate action.

Rationale for appropriate action and further possible actions/commentary for tutorial purposes:

Brianne Ltd	The account balance is not overdue but the customer appears to have exceeded their credit limit. **The customer's ledger account needs to be investigated** to ensure that all transactions have been correctly recorded and that there is no unallocated cash. If the balance is correct, the customer needs to be contacted to explain that no further orders can be processed until some monies have been paid off. We should also bring this to the sales department's attention to ensure that before accepting an order they are checking the credit limit of the customer.
Roxy plc	£2,250 is more than 60 days overdue and as we cannot prove delivery, this **should be allowed for as a doubtful debt**.
Statham and Sons	No cash has been received and it is more than 5 days since the telephone reminder. The fact that the customer said the cheque was in the post suggests there is no query regarding the invoice. **This customer needs to be put on the stop list** (which will result in them receiving an automatic e mail). It may be worth a further telephone call or meeting with customer to establish when payment will be made. A letter needs to be sent threatening legal action if we have not received payment by 10 April X8 when it will be more than 30 days overdue.
Flames Ltd	The invoice has only just become overdue, however the loss of a major customer may severely affect Flame and its ability to pay. We **need to contact them to discuss the situation** and the impact on their business. Potentially they have over £8,000 more credit still available. Given the increased risk **we may need to reconsider their credit status** with us if they are unable to settle on time eg reducing their credit limit to restrict our exposure and possibly tightening the terms. In the meantime we should make the sales department account manager aware of the position and consider an allowance against a portion of Flame's debt.

Ice Ltd	While the payment may relate to £10,000 which is overdue (>60 days) and £5,000 of the 31-60 days debt, we cannot just assume this. It is possible that they were paying all the 31-60 day debt and that £8,000 of the over 60 days debt is in dispute. We **need to contact the customer and ask them to confirm which invoices they were intending to pay** before deciding on appropriate action.

Task 7b

Castle Builders – The amount is more than 60 days overdue and a visit to the customer might be in order to see if we can obtain payment without resort to legal proceedings. If a visit is not successful then legal proceedings should be considered subject to your agreement. As the amount is over 60 days overdue, an allowance should be made for the entire amount.

DD DIY Ltd – A telephone call should be made to remind the company that there is a balance of £1,600 overdue and, in particular, to discover the reason for the amount of £400 that has been overdue for more than 60 days. An allowance might well be necessary for the amount of £400.

AP Partners – £2,250 of the amount outstanding is overdue and £1,250 is over 30 days overdue. The customer should be considered being placed on the stop list and a meeting arranged to clarify the position.

Gatfield Ltd – This appears to be a regular customer but of the total overdue amount of £9,440, £840 is 30 days overdue. A reminder letter and telephone call should be made to the customer and consideration should be given to putting the customer on the stop list. However, as this seems to be a significant customer this should be considered very carefully if other negotiations will suffice.

Kier Ltd – Over half of the amount due from this customer is overdue but also their credit limit appears to have been exceeded. First, the ledger account for this customer should be checked to ensure that all transactions with the customer have been correctly recorded. If this is the case then the customer should be contacted to explain that no further orders can be processed until some monies have been paid to pay off the older debts which will bring the customer back within their credit limit.

Crane Co – There would appear to be no problems with this account.

BPP PRACTICE ASSESSMENT 2
CREDIT CONTROL

Time allowed: 2 hours 30 minutes

Task 1a

Maud goes into a shop and sees a price label for £20 on an ironing board. She takes the board to the checkout but the till operator tells her that the label is misprinted and should read £30. Maud maintains that she only has to pay £20.

How would you describe the price on the price label in terms of contract law?

An offer ☐

A tender ☐

An invitation to treat ☐

An acceptance ☐

Task 1b

Which of the following is not an essential element of a valid simple contract?

The contract must be in writing. ☐

The parties must be in agreement. ☐

Each party must provide consideration. ☐

Each party must intend legal relations. ☐

Task 1c

Samantha offered to sell her car to Patrick for £2,000. She said he could think about it until Monday. Patrick rang her on Saturday and left a message on her machine asking if she would agree to his paying in monthly instalments for six months. She rang back in the evening to say she would want the full cash sum. On Sunday, Patrick accepted the original offer. Meanwhile, Samantha had sold the car to Iain on Saturday night.

What is the legal position?

Patrick's telephone message amounted to a counter-offer which was a final rejection of the original offer. ☐

Patrick's telephone message was a counter-offer but he still had an option on the car until Monday. ☐

Patrick's telephone message was merely a request for information, but as he and Samantha did not yet have agreement, she was free to sell the car to someone else. ☐

Patrick's telephone message was a request for information only, Samantha had not revoked the offer, so his acceptance on the original terms means they have a contract. ☐

Task 1d

In the absence of express statements as to whether or not legal relations are intended which of the following statements is correct?

The courts always assume that legal relations were not intended. ☐

The courts assume that legal relations were not intended unless they were social arrangements. ☐

The courts will assume that legal relations were intended unless the parties can prove otherwise. ☐

The courts assume that legal relations were intended in commercial cases unless proved otherwise. ☐

BPP
LEARNING MEDIA

Task 1e

Which of the following statements concerning contractual terms are correct?

(i) Terms are usually classified as either conditions or warranties.

(ii) If a condition in a contract is not fulfilled the whole contract is said to be discharged by breach.

(iii) If a warranty in a contract is not fulfilled the whole contract is said to be discharged by breach.

(i) only ☐

(ii) only ☐

(i) and, (ii) only ☐

(i) and (iii) only ☐

Task 1f

Which of the following is NOT required for revocation of an offer to be effective?

It must be in writing. ☐

It must be made before the offer is accepted. ☐

It must be made by the offeror or his authorised agent. ☐

It must be communicated to the offeree. ☐

Task 1g

Which of the following statements best describes consideration?

Consideration must be adequate and sufficient. ☐

Consideration must be adequate but need not be sufficient. ☐

Consideration must be sufficient but need not be adequate. ☐

Consideration need be neither sufficient nor adequate. ☐

Task 1h

Which of the following is the normal remedy for breach of contract due to non-payment of a debt?

An action for the goods ☐

Specific performance ☐

Quantum meruit ☐

An action for the price ☐

Task 1i

The Sale of Goods Act 1979 implies a number of terms into consumer contracts. Which of the following are terms it implies?

Title, quantity, fitness ☐

Title, sale by sample, price ☐

Description, price, fitness ☐

Description, quality, fitness ☐

Task 1j

Misrepresentation results in a contract being:

Void ☐

Voidable ☐

Invalid ☐

Valid ☐

BPP
LEARNING MEDIA

Task 1k

Consider the following statements:

(i) The Data Protection Act 1998 applies to computer-based and electronically stored information systems only.

(ii) The Act aims to protect individuals from the use of incorrect information and the misuse of correct, but confidential, information.

Which statements are true?

(i) only ☐

(ii) only ☐

Both (i) and (ii) ☐

Neither statement ☐

Task 1l

Consider the following statements:

(i) A data controller can be either an individual or a company.

(ii) Data is subject to the Data Protection Act's regulation, if it merely records the holder's opinion about the subject, rather than facts about him or her.

Which statements are true?

(i) only ☐

(ii) only ☐

Both statements ☐

Neither statement ☐

Task 2a

When terms of credit are set what is the meaning of "weekly credit"?

The customer must pay by the end of the week in which the invoice was sent. ☐

The customer must pay a week after the invoice was received. ☐

The customer must pay by the end of the week after the invoice was received. ☐

The customer must pay on a specified day in the following week. ☐

Task 2b

Which is the best description of a retention of title clause?

The purchaser has ownership of the goods when they are delivered. ☐

The seller retains ownership of the goods until they are paid for. ☐

The purchaser has ownership of the goods once the invoice is received. ☐

The seller retains ownership of the goods until a cheque is put in the post. ☐

Task 2c

Consider the following statements:

(i)   Insolvency is where an individual cannot pay their debts

(ii)   Under an administrative order a customer must make regular agreed payments into court to pay off a debt

Which statements are true?

(i) only ☐

(ii) only ☐

Both statements ☐

Neither statement

☐

BPP
LEARNING MEDIA

Task 2d

There are a number of remedies available to the injured party for a breach of contract. One is where the court orders one party to the contract **not** to do something.

What is this remedy commonly know as?

Injunction ☐

Termination ☐

Quantum meruit ☐

Specific performance ☐

Task 2e

In the situation where an individual is declared bankrupt, the assets are distributed in a particular order.

Which of the following would receive assets first if assets of the bankrupt were distributed?

Preferential creditors ☐

The bankrupt ☐

Trade payables ☐

Secured creditors ☐

Task 2f

A business currently trades on 30-day credit terms but is considering offering a settlement discount of 2% for payment within seven days of the invoice date.

What is the annual cost of this settlement discount?

2.0% ☐

3.2% ☐

24.8% ☐

32.4% ☐

Task 2g

A business has proposed to increase the credit period that it gives to its customers from one month to two months in order to attract additional customers and increase sales revenue. The current figure for annual sales revenue is £576,000 and the product sells for £15 per unit. It is believed that the introduction of the new credit period will increase sales by an extra 3,600 units. The bank interest cost to the company is 12%.

What is the financing cost of this policy?

£6,840 ☐

£48,000 ☐

£57,000 ☐

£105,000 ☐

Task 2h

Which of the following is not normally a method of collection of debts used by a debt collection agency?

Instigating legal action ☐

Telephone calls ☐

Personal visits ☐

Negotiating payment plans ☐

Task 2i

Which of the following would not be a task of a factoring service which takes over a business's administration of its receivables ledger?

Sending out statements ☐

Assessing credit status ☐

Despatching goods ☐

Sending out invoices ☐

Task 2j

Invoice discounting has which of the following characteristics?

(i) Cheaper form of finance than factoring

(ii) Useful for one-off cash requirements

(iii) Cash provided based on face value of receivables and discount

(i) and (ii) ☐

(i) and (iii) ☐

(ii) and (iii) ☐

All three ☐

Task 3a

Which of the following sources of information would be useful in determining whether to increase the credit limit of an existing credit customer?

(i)   Bank reference

(ii)   Aged receivables' listing

(iii)   Sales representatives knowledge

(iv)   Credit agency reference

(v)   Trade reference

(vi)   Analysis of recent financial statements

(ii), (iii), (iv) and (vi)   ☐

(i), (ii), (v) and (vi)   ☐

(ii), (iii), (v) and (vi)   ☐

(i), (iii), (iv) and (v)   ☐

Task 3b

An organisation has sales of £680,000 and purchases of £330,000. Inventory at the year-end is £45,000 and receivables are £108,000.

What are the figures for inventory turnover and receivables' turnover in days?

Inventory holding period	Accounts receivable collection period	
24 days	58 days	☐
50 days	58 days	☐
50 days	119 days	☐
24 days	119 days	☐

BPP LEARNING MEDIA

Task 3c

Consider the following statements:

(i)   If credit is refused to a customer then this is lost business to the organisation.

(ii)   Credit will only be refused to a customer if the risks are greater than the benefits.

Which statements are correct?

(i) only ☐

(ii) only ☐

Both statements ☐

Neither statement ☐

Task 3d

How is a credit limit for a new customer set?

Based upon their payment of outstanding amounts in the past ☐

Based upon the amount that the customer wishes to purchase ☐

Based upon the risk assessment of the customer ☐

Based upon the recommendation of the sales representatives ☐

Task 3e

A payment from a credit customer for £2,000 has not been entered into the receivables' ledger account for this customer.

Which of the following might be an effect of this error?

(i)   The customer's account could be placed on stop due to exceeding the credit limit.

(ii)   A reminder telephone call might be made to the customer.

(iii)   An allowance for a doubtful debt might be considered.

(i) and (ii) only ☐

(ii) and(iii) only ☐

(i) and (iii) only ☐

All three ☐

Task 4a

You work as a credit control manager for Collins Ltd which uses a credit rating system to assess the credit status of new customers.

The credit rating system table below is used to assess the risk of default by calculating key ratios, comparing them to the table and calculating an aggregate score. The key ratios used are operating profit margin, current ratio, accounts payable payment period, gearing and interest cover.

Credit rating system	Score
Operating profit margin	
Loss	-2
Less than 4%	0
4% to 8%	2
Above 8%	4
Current ratio	
Less than 1 : 1	-2
1: 1 to 2:1	2
Over 2:1	4
Accounts payable payment period	
Up to 30 days	4
30 to 45 days	2
45 to 60 days	0
Over 60 days	-2
Gearing (total debt/(total debt + equity))	
Less than 30%	4
Between 30% and 50%	2
Between 50% and 70%	0
Over 70%	-2

BPP
LEARNING MEDIA

Credit rating system	Score
Interest cover	
No cover	-2
Less than 1	0
Between 1 and 3	2
Over 3	4
Risk assessment	
Very low risk	16 to 20
Low risk	10 to 15
Medium risk	5 to 9
High risk	0 to 4
Very high risk	-10 to 0

The sales department has asked for a credit limit of £20,000 for Oxford Ltd who is a potential new credit customer. Oxford Ltd has provided the following financial statements.

Summarised statements of profit or loss

	Year ending 31 December		
	20X8	20X7	20X6
	£'000	£'000	£'000
Sales revenue	2,660	2,570	2,520
Cost of sales	1,690	1,650	1,640
Gross profit	**970**	**920**	**880**
Operating expenses	580	540	510
Profit from operations	**390**	**380**	**370**
Finance costs (Interest payable)	90	80	75
Profit from operations before tax	**300**	**300**	**295**
Tax	72	76	72
Profit for the financial year	**228**	**224**	**223**

Summarised statements of financial position

	As at 31 December		
	20X8	20X7	20X6
	£'000	£'000	£'000
ASSETS			
Non-current assets	3,741	3,380	3,029
Current assets:			
Inventory	280	260	230
Trade receivables	550	540	510
Cash at bank	2	3	4
	832	803	744
Total assets	4,573	4,183	3,773
EQUITY AND LIABILITES			
Equity			
Ordinary share capital	800	800	800
Retained earnings	1,715	1,487	1,263
Total equity	2,515	2,287	2,063
Non-current liabilities			
Borrowings (long-term loans)	1,600	1,400	1,200
Current liabilities			
Trade payables	370	380	395
Other payables	88	116	125
	458	496	510
Total liabilities	2,058	1,896	1,710
Total equity and liabilities	4,573	4,183	3,773

Using the templates provided

(i)   Calculate the key ratios for each of the three years for Oxford Ltd (to 2dp), and

(ii)   Rate the company using the credit rating (scoring) system.

	Indicator	Rating	Indicator	Rating	Indicator	Rating
	20X8		20X7		20X6	
Operating profit margin (%)						
Current ratio (:1)						
Accounts payable payment period (days)						
Gearing (%)						
Interest cover (times)						
Total						

Task 4b

Based on the results of your credit rating, recommend, with reasons, whether the requested credit limit should be given to Oxford Ltd.

Task 5a

You are the credit controller for Glenn Ltd and you have received a request for £30,000 of credit from a potential new customer, TG Ltd. TG Ltd has provided you with its latest set of financial statements which are summarised below:

Statements of profit or loss for the years ended 30 June

	20X9	20X8
	£'000	£'000
Revenue	1,920	1,800
Cost of sales	1,490	1,400
Gross profit	**430**	**400**
Operating expenses	180	160
Profit from operations	**250**	**240**
Finance costs	56	38
Profit from operations before tax	**194**	**202**
Taxation	39	44
Profit for the financial year	**155**	**158**

Statements of financial position at 30 June

	20X9	20X8
	£'000	£'000
ASSETS		
Non-current assets	**2,610**	**2,290**
Current assets		
Inventory	210	170
Trade receivables	270	280
	480	450
Total assets	**3,090**	**2,740**
EQUITY AND LIABILITIES		
Equity		
Share capital	1,200	1,200
Retained earnings	1,015	860
Total equity	**2,215**	**2,060**
Current liabilities		
Trade payables	305	300
Bank overdraft	570	380
Total liabilities	**875**	**680**
Total equity and liabilities	**3,090**	**2,740**

Calculate the following financial ratios for TG Ltd to 2dp:

	20X9	20X8
Gross profit margin (%)		
Operating profit margin (%)		
Return on capital employed (%)		
Asset turnover		
Current ratio (:1)		
Quick ratio (:1)		
Inventory holding period (days)		
Accounts receivable collection period (days)		
Accounts payable payment period (days)		
Interest cover (times)		

Task 5b

Using the information from Task 1.5a, complete the following memo (using dropdown boxes or by entering a number to the nearest whole number) assessing the financial statements of TG provided, reaching a conclusion as to the level of credit that should be extended to them.

Memo

Subject: Request for credit from TG Ltd

After the request from TG Ltd for £30,000 of credit I have examined the information that we have available about the company which includes the financial statements for the last two years.

Financial statements

The financial statements for TG Ltd for the last two years have been examined and the key ratios calculated under the headings of profitability, liquidity and gearing.

Although the company appears to be (1) [_____] ▼ there is some concern about the company's (2) [_____].

Both the current and quick ratios are (3) [_____]. ▼

The company appears to have been financed for the last two years by a (4) [_____] ▼ . The interest cover in 20X9 is (5) [_____] ▼ at over [____] times.

The payables' payment period is [____] days. Although it has (6) [_____] ▼ , it is (7) [_____] ▼ than the company's receivables' collection period.

This could be (8) [_____] ▼ .

Conclusion

In the absence of any further information I suggest that we (9)

[_____] ▼

BPP LEARNING MEDIA

Picklists – commentary on ratios

(1) Liquid/profitable

(2) Liquidity/profitability

(3) Seemingly very low and are decreasing/seemingly very high and are increasing/seemingly very low and are increasing/seeming very low and are decreasing

(4) Long term loan/substantial overdraft

(5) Reasonably healthy/very unhealthy

(6) Risen by 4%/fallen by 4%/risen by 10%/fallen by 10%

(7) Much longer/much shorter

(8) A sign the company's cash flow is improving/a sign of overtrading

(9) Offer TG Ltd the £30,000 credit they have requested/offer TG Ltd a trial period of credit at a lower level (eg £10,000) until further information is obtained/refuse TG Ltd credit

....

Task 6

Carmen Contractors Ltd is an existing customer and has been for many years. Carmen has requested that your company, FH Panels, extend Carmen's credit limit from £10,000 to £20,000. The company has provided its statements of profit or loss for each of the two years ended 31 March 20X5 and 20X6 and statements of financial position as at those dates.

Carmen Contractors Ltd: Statements of profit or loss for the years ending 31 March

	20X6	20X5
	£'000	£'000
Revenue	5,600	5,000
Cost of sales	4,400	4,000
Gross profit	**1,200**	**1,000**
Operating expenses	850	800
Profit from operations	**350**	**200**
Finance costs	100	100
Profit from operations before tax	**250**	**100**
Taxation	80	20
Profit for the financial year	**170**	**80**

Carmen Contractors Ltd: Statements of Financial Position for year ending 31 March:

	20X6	20X5
	£'000	£'000
ASSETS		
Non-current assets	**2,150**	**1,940**
Current assets		
Inventory	420	400
Trade receivables	220	140
	640	**540**
Total assets	**2,790**	**2,480**
EQUITY AND LIABILITIES		
Equity		
Share capital	800	800
Retained earnings	380	210
Total equity	**1,180**	**1,010**
Current liabilities		
Trade payables	560	520
Overdraft	1,050	950
Total liabilities	**1,610**	**1,470**
Total equity and liabilities	**2,790**	**2,480**

Prepare a report for your supervisor analysing the results of Carmen Contractors for the last two years and concluding on whether the credit limit for the company should be extended as requested by Carmen.

Task 7a

The debt collection policy and extract from the aged receivables' analysis and supporting customer notes, are set out below.

DEBT COLLECTION POLICY

Invoices must be sent out the day after the goods/service is provided.

All customers are required to pay within 30 days of the invoice date.

An aged receivables' analysis is produced monthly.

Statements are sent to all customers in the first week of each month.

When a debt is seven days overdue a telephone call is made to the customer.

When a debt is 14 days overdue a reminder letter is sent to the customer.

If a debt becomes 30 days overdue the customer is put on the stop list and a meeting with the customer is arranged.

When a debt is 60 days overdue it is put into the hands of a debt collector.

When a debt is 90 days overdue legal proceedings are commenced subject to the agreement of the managing director.

Aged receivables' analysis at 30 June 20X9 – extract

Customer	Amount due	Current	31 to 60 days	61 to 90 days	> 90 days
	£	£	£	£	£
Havanna Ltd	11,250		11,250		
Jones Partners	8,000			8,000	
Norman Bros	11,100	10,700	400		
Kiera Ltd	23,000	12,000	10,000		1,000

Notes

- The outstanding invoice for Havanna Ltd is dated 20 May 20X9.

- The outstanding invoice for Jones Partners is dated 14 April 20X9.

- The invoices for Norman Bros were dated as follows:

  - £10,700 12 June 20X9

  - £400 17 May 20X9 – a telephone call was made on 28 June to chase this debt but there has been no response

- The invoice to Kiera Ltd for £1,000 which is over 90 days old is in dispute as the customer claims that the goods were faulty and returned them. Kiera Ltd is a long-

standing customer with a generally good record for paying although always takes longer than the 30 days credit period.

For each customer, select the appropriate credit control action that is required for these customers.

Customer	Action	
Havanna Ltd		▼
Jones Partners		▼
Norman Bros		▼
Kiera Ltd		▼

Picklists:

Havanna Ltd

No action is required

This customer should be sent a reminder letter now

A telephone call should be made to the Havanna to remind them payment is due

Jones Partners

A meeting should be arranged with the customer and the account should be put on the stop list.

The account need not be put on the stop list but a telephone call should be made requesting payment

No action is necessary

The debt should be put in the hands of the debt collector

Norman Bros

The account should be put on the stop list

The account need not be put on the stop list but a follow up telephone call should be made requesting immediate payment for £400

A reminder letter needs to be sent in relation to the £400 and a phone call made in relation to the remaining £10,700

No action is required in relation to the £10,700 but a reminder letter should be sent in relation to the £400

No action is required as £400 is such a small proportion of the total amount outstanding

Kiera Ltd

No action is necessary

Check that the dispute is genuine by calling Kiera and checking returned goods records

Commence legal action

Put the account on the stop list until payment is received

Task 7b

An extract of the aged receivables' analysis and the company's credit control policy is set out below.

AGED RECEIVABLES' ANALYSIS

Customer	Amount due £	Current £	31–60 days £	61–90 days £	91 + day £
Candles Ltd	12,500.65				12,500.65
Lux Ltd	3,250.00	2,250.00	850.00		150.00
Lights Ltd	1,475.00		475.00	1,000.00	
Flames Ltd	16,815.75	9,275.50	6,120.25	1,420.00	

CREDIT CONTROL POLICY

1.   Invoices must be issued on the same day as goods are despatched.

2.   An aged analysis of trade receivables is to be produced monthly.

3.   Statements are to be despatched on the first working day of each month.

4.   A reminder letter must be sent when a debt is 14 days overdue.

5.   A telephone call to chase payment must be made when a debt is 21 days overdue.

6.   The customer will be placed on the stop list when the debt is 30 days overdue and a meeting arranged with the customer to discuss the operation of the account.

7.   A letter threatening legal action will be sent when the debt is 45 days overdue.

8.   Legal proceedings to be commenced when a debt is 60 days overdue, subject to agreement with the financial controller.

BPP
LEARNING MEDIA

Using the information above:

- Set out the action to be taken with regard to each of the four customer accounts
- State how discussion should be conducted with overdue accounts
- Recommend whether any allowances for doubtful debts are required

BPP
LEARNING MEDIA

BPP PRACTICE ASSESSMENT 2
CREDIT CONTROL

ANSWERS

BPP PRACTICE ASSESSMENT 2
CREDIT CONTROL

ANSWERS

Task 1a

The correct answer is: An invitation to treat

A price label, or even a display of goods, is an invitation to the customer to make an offer which the shop may then choose to accept. It is an invitation to treat.

....

Task 1b

The correct answer is: The contract must be in writing.

....

Task 1c

The correct answer is: Patrick's telephone message was a request for information only, Samantha had not revoked the offer, so his acceptance on the original terms means they have a contract.

Patrick's query is only a query as to whether other terms would be acceptable, that is, a request for information. Samantha responded to that request for information but her response is not a revocation of her original offer. As she has not revoked her offer, it is still open for Patrick to accept. This means that on Sunday, Patrick and Samantha have a contract.

....

Task 1d

The correct answer is: The courts assume that legal relations were intended in commercial cases unless proved otherwise.

....

Task 1e

The correct answer is: (i) and, (ii) only

....

Task 1f

The correct answer is: It must be in writing.

Revocation may be express or implied, and made orally or in writing. The important thing is that it is communicated to the offeree before acceptance.

....

Task 1g

The correct answer is: Consideration must be sufficient but need not be adequate.

Consideration must have some identifiable value ('sufficient') but does not need to be equal in value to the consideration received in return ('adequate').

Task 1h

The correct answer is: An action for the price

Task 1i

The correct answer is: Description, quality, fitness

Task 1j

The correct answer is: Voidable

Task 1k

The correct answer is: (ii) only

The Act also applies to manual files.

Task 1l

The correct answer is: Both statements

Task 2a

The correct answer is: The customer must pay on a specified day in the following week.

Task 2b

The correct answer is: The seller retains ownership of the goods until they are paid for.

BPP
LEARNING MEDIA

Task 2c

The correct answer is: (ii) only

Task 2d

The correct answer is: Injunction

Task 2e

The correct answer is: Secured creditors

Task 2f

The correct answer is: 32.4%

Cost of discount $= \dfrac{2}{100-2} \times \dfrac{365}{30-7} \times 100$

$ = 32.4\%$

Task 2g

The correct answer is: £6,840

Current receivables	=	£576,000/12
	=	£48,000
New sales revenue	=	£576,000 + (3,600 × £15)
	=	£630,000
New receivables	=	£630,000 × 2/12
	=	£105,000
Increase in receivables	=	£57,000
Cost of increase	=	£57,000 × 12%
	=	£6,840

Task 2h

The correct answer is: Instigating legal action

Task 2i

The correct answer is: Despatching goods

Task 2j

The correct answer is: (ii) and (iii)

Task 3a

The correct answer is: (ii), (iii), (iv) and (vi)

Task 3b

The correct answer is: Inventory holding period = 50 days, Accounts receivable collection period = 58 days.

Task 3c

The correct answer is: (ii) only

The refusal of credit does not necessarily mean a loss of the business as the customer may choose to trade on cash terms.

Task 3d

The correct answer is: Based upon the risk assessment of the customer

---

BPP
LEARNING MEDIA

Task 3e

The correct answer is: (i) and (ii) only

It is unlikely that an allowance for a doubtful debt would be made without further evidence of a problem.

••

Task 4a

(i)   Oxford Ltd

(ii)

	Indicator	Rating	Indicator	Rating	Indicator	Rating
	20X8		20X7		20X6	
Operating profit margin (%)	14.66%	4	14.79%	4	14.68%	4
Current ratio (:1)	1.82	2	1.62	2	1.46	2
Accounts payable payment period (days)	79.91	-2	84.06	-2	87.91	-2
Gearing (%)	38.88	2	37.97	2	36.78	2
Interest cover (times)	4.33	4	4.75	4	4.93	4
Total		10		10		10

••

Task 4b

The credit rating indicates that Oxford Ltd is a low risk customer and therefore the credit limit requested should be granted. However, when considering the credit rating in more detail there is some concern about the payables' turnover which at 80 days or more is considerably higher than our credit terms of 30 days. Therefore credit should be granted to Oxford Ltd on a trial basis for six months but with strictly 30 days credit terms.

••

BPP LEARNING MEDIA

Task 5a

	20X9	20X8
Gross profit margin (%)	22.40	22.22
Operating profit margin (%)	13.02	13.33
Return on capital employed (%)	11.29	11.65
Asset turnover	0.87	0.87
Current ratio (:1)	0.55	0.66
Quick ratio (:1)	0.31	0.41
Inventory holding period (days)	51.44	44.32
Accounts receivable collection period (days)	51.33	56.78
Accounts payable payment period (days)	74.71	78.21
Interest cover (times)	4.46	6.32

BPP LEARNING MEDIA

Task 5b

> **Memo**
>
> Subject: Request for credit from TG Ltd
>
> After the request from TG Ltd for £30,000 of credit I have examined the information that we have available about the company which includes the financial statements for the last two years.
>
> **Financial statements**
>
> The financial statements for TG Ltd for the last two years have been examined and the key ratios calculated under the headings of profitability, liquidity and gearing.
>
> Although the company appears to be **profitable** there is some concern about the company's **liquidity**. Both the current and quick ratios are **seemingly very low and are decreasing**. The company appears to have been financed for the last two years by a **substantial overdraft**. The interest cover is **reasonably healthy** at over **4** times.
>
> The payables' payment period is **75** days. Although it has **fallen by 4%**, it is **much longer** than the company's receivables' collection period. This could be **a sign of overtrading**.
>
> **Conclusion**
>
> In the absence of any further information I suggest that we **offer TG Ltd a trial period of credit at a lower level (eg £10,000) until further information is obtained**.

Task 6

REPORT

To: Supervisor   From: Accounting Technician

Date:

Subject: Carmen Contractors Ltd – request for extension of credit limit

I have analysed the financial statements provided by Carmen Contractors Ltd for the years ending 31 March 20X5 and 20X6. The results of this analysis are set out below.

Profitability

Revenues have grown significantly during the year (by 12%). The gross profit margin has increased from 20% in 20X5 to 21.4% in 20X6. Both these increases have played a part in the increase in operating profit and the operating profit margin, increasing from 4% to 6.3%. Even though asset turnover has decreased slightly the significant increase in profit from operations has led to an impressive increase in return on capital employed (20X6: 29.7%, 20X5: 19.8%), increasing by almost 10%. The profitability indicators are therefore positive, however these need to be considered together with key liquidity indicators.

Liquidity

The company appears to operate with very low levels of liquidity with low figures for both the current ratio (0.4) and the quick ratio (0.1). This would appear to be largely due to very low levels of receivables and being financed by a large overdraft, which has increased by £100,000 during the year. The fact that the increased profits have not been converted to an improved cash position can probably be explained by the increased capital expenditure (non-current assets have increased by £210,000), and increasing inventory levels.

Of particular interest to us (as potential payables of the company) is their accounts payable payment period which has remained at around 46 to 47 days. As we offer only 30 days of credit then this is of some concern.

Interest cover

The business is heavily financed by a bank overdraft with the related interest charges. Interest cover was low in 20X5 at 2 times, but has improved in 20X6 to 3.5 times which is an encouraging sign, although this is due to improving profits since the overdraft itself increased and there was no fall in interest payable.

Summary and conclusion

Although profitability is improving, there are some causes for concern over the liquidity of the business. The revenue growth, taken together with the apparent capital expenditure, payables payment period and deteriorating cash position could be an indication Carmen is overtrading, and it would therefore be risky to increase the credit limit at this time.

The request to increase the credit limit to £20,000 should be refused until further investigation can be carried out.

BPP
LEARNING MEDIA

Summary of ratios for information

	20X6	20X5
Gross profit margin	21.4%	20.0%
Operating profit margin	6.3%	4.0%
Return on capital employed	29.7%	19.8%
Asset turnover	4.75	4.95
Current ratio	0.4 : 1	0.4 : 1
Quick (acid test) ratio	0.1 : 1	0.1 : 1
Inventory holding period	35 days	37 days
Accounts receivable collection period	14 days	10 days
Accounts payable payment period	46 days	47 days
Interest cover	3.5 times	2.0 times

Task 7a

Customer	Action
Havanna Ltd	A telephone call should be made to the Havanna to remind them payment is due
Jones Partners	A meeting should be arranged with the customer and the account should be put on the stop list.
Norman Bros	No action is required in relation to the £10,700 but a reminder letter should be sent in relation to the £400
Kiera Ltd	Check that the dispute is genuine by calling Kiera and checking returned goods records

Rationale for appropriate action and further possible actions/commentary for tutorial purposes:

Havanna Ltd	This debt is now 11 days overdue and a telephone call should be made to the customer. It should be pointed out that the debt for £11,250 is now overdue and it should be established whether there is any query with regard to the debt. If there is no query then a date for payment should be established. If there is a problem with this amount then consideration should be given to making an allowance.
Jones Partners	This debt is now more than 30 days overdue and therefore the customer should be put on the stop list and no further credit sales made to this customer. A meeting with the customer should also be arranged in order to establish when the amount of £800 is to be paid. An allowance for this amount should probably be made.
Norman Bros	The debt of £10,700 is not yet overdue but the debt for £400 is 14 days overdue and there has been no response to the telephone call made on 28 June. Therefore a strongly but courteously worded reminder letter should be sent to the customer stating the amount that is overdue of £400 and that payment should be sent within seven days or further action will be taken.
Kiera Ltd	It would appear that the dispute with Kiera Ltd is genuine but this must be checked with a telephone call and checking the records of returned goods. If this amount is a genuine dispute then it will probably need to be written-off as an irrecoverable debt given the customer's record of paying in the past.

Task 7b

Action to be taken with customer accounts

Candles Ltd

We need to consider if we should visit the company to see if we can obtain payment without legal action. If a visit does not prove satisfactory, I recommend legal proceedings be commenced on this overdue debt, subject to your agreement. We should create an allowance for the whole balance of £12,500.65 due from Candles Ltd as it is more than 60 days overdue.

Lux Ltd

We should phone the company to remind them of the overdue balance of £1,000, and also to clarify the position regarding the £150 that is more than 60 days overdue. Non-payment may be due to a specific invoice that is in dispute, or which has been misposted. No allowance is necessary at present.

Lights Ltd

All of the balance of £1,475 is overdue and £1,000 is more than 30 days overdue. We should consider placing this customer on stop and should arrange a meeting to discuss the operation of the account. No allowance is necessary at present.

Flames Ltd

We should remind this customer by phone of the overdue balances of £7,540.25, out of a total balance of £16,815.75. We should consider placing the customer on stop because the balance of £1,420 has been outstanding for more than 30 days. However, as the customer seems to be doing a lot of business with us, we need to consider the dangers of losing this trade, and only act if the balance more than 30 days overdue increases further. No allowance is necessary at present.

BPP
LEARNING MEDIA